To Rachel

Best Wishes

RISE BEFORE YOUR BULL

RISE BEFORE YOUR BULL

AND OTHER HABITS OF SUCCESSFUL PEOPLE

Ciara Conlon

Ballpoint Press

For J, My Sunshine

Published in 2019 by Ballpoint Press
4 Wyndham Park, Bray,
Co Wicklow, Republic of Ireland

Telephone: 00353 86 821 7631
Email: ballpointpress1@gmail.com
Web: www.ballpointpress.ie

ISBN 978–1–9998306–7–0

Book design and production by Joe Coyle Media&Design,
joecoyledesign@gmail.com

Printed and bound in Ireland by SPRINT-print Ltd.

Contents

Acknowledgements

TO Johnny Clegg, the inspiration to *Rise Before My Bull* and a joyful addition to many evenings.

Thank you to PJ Cunningham, whose support and encouragement go far beyond your role as publisher. To Joe Coyle of Joe Coyle Design for turning my words into this book.

Introduction

SOMETIME in 2006, I sat slumped on my living-room floor, probably suffering from post-natal depression. With three boys, two of them still toddlers, I was finding life tough. My 10-year-old came down the stairs into the living room and asked: "Are you alright mum?"

"Yes, yes I'm fine I just have to get every one dressed and get out for a walk," I replied. What he said to me next changed me forever; "It's not because you have to mum, it's because you want to."

"Not because I have to, because I want to."

These words have shaped my life ever since. I realised that the life I was living was my choice, that staying on the living-room floor or going for a walk was my decision, the latter leading to more positive results. How we choose to spend each day is our choice and the totality of those choices add up to give us the life we are living right now.

When you understand that everything in life is a decision within your control and that you have the power to affect it, you can stop the cycle of playing the victim. Self-pity becomes obsolete and self-empowerment becomes addictive. One of the ways you stay stuck in victim mode is when you listen to the negative disempowering thoughts that want you to stay where you are, the thoughts that will make you resist change and progress. This book will help you to uncover those thoughts and become the master of them.

That day I decided to make changes in my life, I started to make better choices and those small inches added up to give me better results. I got organised, started to look after my health and fitness and did the things that I knew would bring more joy into my life.

This book is a culmination of the lessons I've learnt from that day forward. It didn't happen overnight and I gradually changed my life from minor depression, self-pity and feeling powerless to achieving my goals, making a success of my life and finding happiness.

I have devised a methodology for creating habits that will get you to your goals. By focusing on the smallest parts, you can create a big impact. By changing one thing at a time, you can stop feeling disappointed in yourself, start finding time where you think there is none and take action towards being the person you always knew you could be.

Not long ago I was the person who sat slumped on the floor, the person who drank to find distraction, ate due to boredom and envied the runners and gym-goers. I have now taken control of my bad habits and mastered many good habits.

In the following pages, I will share with you the methods that can transform you from feeling dejected and frustrated to being satisfied and yes, even proud. I know they work because they have helped many people unlock their potential and reach their goals.

By mastering your daily habits, you can master your life.

PART 1

Transforming The Old To The New

What many didn't realise was that the chief had a custom, a strategy that had worked for his forefathers before him

1

The Chief And His Bull

THIS story begins with a bull and a Zulu chief. The chief, a small wiry figure who without his ceremonial garb could be confused for an ageing beggar, was a well respected man. His rough and wrinkled skin not too distinct from the rhino that grazed near by, appeared to have stood the test of time, as his age nobody could tell. His people, when asked, did not remember a time when the chief was not chief nor a time when the chief looked any different than he did today. His physical demeanour did not take from his station, revered by all, he was a clever man who knew of the necessity to stay one step ahead of his tribe. The chief carried out his chiefly duties each day with pride and grace. Making decisions for the good of the tribe, negotiating with the chiefs of other tribes and generally looking after the health and wellbeing of his kin.

He was a fair and just leader and maintained order with ease. He respected the council and sought out their advice in times of hardship, but ultimately, it was he who made all the difficult decisions. The decisions that would protect the welfare of all who were in his charge.

What many didn't realise was that the chief had a custom, a strategy that had worked for his forefathers before him. This custom was adopted by each chief, none questioned its rationale and all instinctively understood its value. Every morning he would wake in that time of day when night is no longer king, when there is a hint of a different ruler on the horizon. Our chief would stand up with such quiet that he never disturbed the sleeping bodies of his family that surrounded him and walk out of his hut.

As the dawn approached he walked away from his people, his animals and all that he reigned to the boundary of his territory. Where the sky meets the land with a red hue, there his figure could be seen, that is, if there were open eyes to witness him. A legendary figure outlined by light on the horizon, standing strong with the knowing that this ritual was how and why he maintained the respect of all who knew him. And as the amber liquid left his body he sighed, a knowing sigh that once again his rule remained intact. He knew that his morning ritual of waking before even his prize bull had stirred was what made him chief. He was ahead of the masses, he stayed in control because he was the one to "pee before his bull".

This story is one I heard recounted many years ago at an open-air music concert in Cape Town, South Africa. While I may have embellished or even completely rewritten the story, its essence was told by Johnny Clegg, a musician and anthropologist born in England but brought up in his mother's native land of Zimbabwe. The story resonated with me back then, as at that time I was attempting to improve yet again the quality of my life and in particular trying to change the habit of a lifetime, and start *rising before my bull*.

Are You Ready To Cut The Bull?

Just like the Zulu chief had a morning ritual, I too had one but it didn't keep me in control; my ritual kept me stuck in a place I didn't want to be. Instead of rising before my bull, I lay there and listened to it. This bull was the one that was ruling my life, the bull inside my head. Line after line of self-sabotaging dialogue, telling me I was a failure, that I wasn't good enough to be successful, that I would never be rich. All of the repetitive thoughts that gave me the excuse to stay stuck. I had thousands of creative excuses to avoid rising early; I went to bed too late, I need more sleep, I think I'm catching a cold, I'll be too tired at work today if I exercise now.

But then I realised this bull wasn't limited just to the morning... it went on all day. It prevented me from eating the food I knew I wanted to eat, from exercising, from meditating, from believing in myself and in my ability to help others. These thoughts were predominantly of self-pity and disappointment and it had to stop.

The day I figured out how to 'Rise Before My Bull' was the day I took control of my life. More than that – it freed me to finally and authentically help others to take control of theirs.

When I started out as a coach I helped many people to reach their goals, I advised them to practise gratitude, positivity and productivity. I guided them to break down their goals into smaller parts and schedule them, while giving them tips on how to continuously take action. I looked at their individual challenges and blocks and advised them how to avoid the typical obstacles that trip up even the most invested.

However, I spent little or no time talking to them about the true essence of goal-setting, the smallest of parts that make up our goals, big and small. It was years later through mastering my own habits that I realised by focusing on these smaller parts, our daily habits, we can impact big lasting change.

Habit is core to who you are. The quality of your life can be related back to the quality of your daily habits. Everything you do each day contributes to the quality of the life you are living today. Your daily habits determine your state of being and ultimately your personality. Habits can be responsible for negative or self-defeating behaviour or habits can be supportive, positive behaviours that improve your health, wealth and happiness.

Our habits make us who we are.

A popular radio presenter in Ireland, Dave Fanning, once asked me in an interview: "Ciara, what if you don't want to change?"

My answer that day was: "Wonderful, if you are happy with who you are, then there is no need to change." I later realised that I hadn't answered that question the way I should have, because the reality is very different. Truth is, if you don't have a desire to change, you are not growing and there are very few people in the world who have reached a point where growth or change is not desired in some way.

According to the World Health Organisation, 350 million adults suffer from depression. Unhappiness and being dissatisfied with life have become the resting state for too far many people. Why are so many adults, the majority of them living in first world countries, suffering when they don't have to be? Many of these individuals will need professional help but there are also millions of people who could change their state of happiness by taking back the control of their own life.

So even if you are just like Dave and don't have grand goals of transformation, I'm sure you do want to be healthier, slimmer, more mindful or happier. Changing your daily habits can help you become these things and more. I'm sure also you have negative habits that you would like to exclude from your daily routine. By recognising your current habits and deciding whether they are supporting you to reach your goals or not, is the first step in changing your life for the better. Only when you shine a light on the current situation can you take steps towards positive change.

I Am Who I Am

But wait a minute, I hear you say, what if you're doomed by your DNA? Maybe your personality restricts you from being a calmer person or a slimmer version of who you currently are? Maybe you are clumsy or self-conscious or a bad listener. You may have tried to change before and failed, reinforcing your belief that well... you are who you are.

Take me — I am a redhead, so the assumption will go that I'm short-tempered, quick to anger. While those assumptions may hold true, being defined in this way only reinforces my behaviour when it does occur. I can be calm, relaxed and peaceful and meditation has helped me to smile at teenage behaviour rather than get triggered by it. I also have a tendency towards chaos, mess and disorder but that does not mean I have to live my life that way. My first two books, 'Chaos to Control', a practical guide to getting things done and my second publication, 'Productivity for Dummies', were books that taught me as much, if not more than my readers. By learning new skills and deliberately creating new habits, I have managed to change my natural behaviours and not let them negatively effect my life and the lives of those around me.

Not only has meditation helped me to stay calm, it also helps me to focus better. That, combined with productivity habits, changed my life from a place of frustration and under-achievement to one where I can realise my goals. Write books, study, run a Leadership Development consultancy and raise three boys all of which have contributed to my more fulfilled and happier life. New habits such as planning my weeks and days and focusing on my priorities enabled me to stop playing victim to the person thought I was and create the 'me' I wanted to become.

If you have hidden behind your personality up to now, explaining your behaviours as innate and out of your control, I'm going to unmask the truth and tell you that your personality traits and behavioural habits can be changed. It just needs a desire and a conscious effort to be the person you long to be.

Habits are your pathway to success in life. Whatever it is you want to achieve, whoever it is you want to be, it all requires positive habits to help you get there. So if you are ready to stop making excuses and take action, read on.

What Exactly Is Habit?

Habits can be explained as a physical or mental activity that we do without having to think. They are routine behaviours that have become automated. So when habits are formed they are often enacted without conscious intent. Our habits are believed to be controlled from the most primitive part of the brain, the basal ganglia. When we repeat our actions regularly the neural networks in our brain make stronger connections until we form a habit.

As we are all too aware this can be a blessing and a curse at the same time, great if it involves the gym or the lotus pose but not so great if it involves a Homer pose with a can of Duff beer. When the connections are formed they are strong — strong enough to resist change even when the intentions are good. This is not helpful when we have habits that aren't good for us or are damaging to our health and happiness. So while it is positive to know that we can learn new habits, we also have to 'unlearn' the bad habits that have held us back.

Have you ever found yourself in front of the fridge at a certain time of the day without being hungry? Do you bite your nails or smoke a cigarette or have a drink when you are feeling stressed? These are all habits we have created without being conscious of the fact it was happening. Why are these habits so easily formed when the habit of working out is one you just can't seem to master?

It's not necessarily that these habits were easily formed just that you have repeated the behaviour so often that it is easier to follow the path most travelled then carve out a new one. This book will show you how to carve new paths that will help you reach your pot of gold at the end of the rainbow.

Habits And Goals

Normally when people make a conscious decision to form a positive habit, they are aiming to reach a new goal in life. If you decided to take up running to become healthier, to achieve this goal running must become a habit. If you don't commit to running a number of days a week, chances are you won't form a lasting habit and you won't achieve your goal. Each of us has hundreds of habits that we play out each day. We drink cups of tea at the same time, we shower, read, write, work, watch TV all habitual behaviours that have become semi-automated in our lives. We also have habitual thoughts that we replay over and over and sometimes replacing these can be more life-changing than anything.

Creating new habits involves change and that can only happen when a level of personal awareness is reached. We need to be consciously aware of what it is we are trying to change and what our desired end result is. Clear outcomes drive us towards achievement and without the clear picture of what they may be, the path tends be a little rockier en route. Over the years I have tried to create habits... without success. Often it was because I was aiming for something I thought I should be doing because everybody else was.

When you try to create a habit without having real desire, you are setting yourself up for disappointment. When you are aiming to create new goals or start new habits, the more passionate or motivated you are personally towards achieving them, the more likely you will succeed.

Over the past 10 years I've been a student of habit; it has intrigued me how some personalities create new habits easier than others, how some maintain new habits easily and others repeatedly drop them only to start again weeks or months later. We appear to crave the security yet resist the constraint. The truth is we often resist what we need most.

My Story

I was never one for good habits. I am the youngest of six children. My brother was the eldest, followed by five sisters, each one a possible male companion for my brother but each time a little more pink arrived. My mother always said he was never disappointed, always excited by the new life, until the next pregnancy and the next possibility. Ten years on and 10 days overdue, it had been unanimously agreed that this one had to be the boy, as all the sisters had arrived early. So confident in their prediction, that they called me Joe. The long awaited brother finally popped out in less than an hour and once again the excitement of new life overshadowed the truth of my female form.

I believe this early conditioning had an effect on my life that followed — I never liked to blend in with others. While not adverse to playing with dolls and dressing up, I also wanted to play with cars and build things. I saw myself as being a bit different, conforming with society's tradition and the status quo were very low on my agenda. Most importantly I never liked to be told what to do.

As a child I'd drop my toys to play with snails.

When other teenagers received chocolates and flowers from their boyfriends on Valentine's Day, I asked for a goldfish, called Clayton.

College taught me neither discipline nor routine. My journey to college took me two and half hours each morning. Early economics lectures didn't fit with my image of college life. I failed economics that year. Telling them I wasn't a morning person didn't seem to help my case.

For many years I continued to hate mornings, routines and structure and becoming a mother at 24 wasn't going to change me. As a young mother whose friends continued to go out partying and having fun, I didn't want to be left behind, so I avoided sticking to routines. I brought my little boy everywhere. I continued to live the life of a young single person. I never admitted that I was making my life more difficult by not giving a child routine and structure. Two more children didn't change my stubborn ways. I learnt the hard way. It took many years for me to see that I was spending so much energy avoiding normal daily routine that there was little left over to create a happy life.

Fortunately things were about to change and it all started with breaking the habit of a lifetime. My allergy to mornings started early; maybe it was the cold bedrooms of my youth or the lack of motivation to get to school in the morning, whatever it was, I had it bad. I suffered from this allergy most of life. I heard leadership expert Robin Sharma put the call out to join his 5am club. He said it was a club for those who want to achieve greatness. To be extraordinary he said one must model the habits of the rich and successful. Did I want to be one of the people to take action and make big change happen?

Yes, yes I did but once again I wanted to do it on my terms.

I rationalised that all of the habits he suggested doing in the morning like exercise and meditation I could do at any time of the day. But the thing was — I wasn't doing them. Not at 5am nor at 10am, there was no time for these habits in the midst of the chaos of self-employment and motherhood.

But even though I resisted, rising early became an object of my attention for some time. It showed up in song lyrics and on the covers of books. It showed up at music concerts and in the stories of famous men and women of history. It persisted in the form of the early riser that slept beside me each night. But having it always in my conscious mind wasn't enough to make me do anything about it. I got good at adding to the million reasons why being an early riser wasn't right for me. Why did I need to get out of my cocoon at an ungodly hour to reach greatness? Subconsciously though I understood that rising early was my next step to greatness, but I couldn't quite get agreement from the rest of my body.

I made my first attempt after reading the fact that the difference between rising at 5am and 7am everyday for 40 years adds up to 10 years of your life. The shock of how much of my life I was wasting tempted me to change my life-long habit. So with the temptation of elongating my life, I decided to give it a go.

So give it a go I did, and another go... and another. I would do it for two days in a row and then have an excuse for not doing it the next. My bank of excuses was limitless and I quite happily dipped into it when I wanted a day off. I was up too late last night...I'm feeling a little ill... the kids disturbed my sleep last night... I'll just take one day off.

Even after training to be a coach, studying personality profiles and understanding more about myself and others, I continued to suffer in creating habits. I learned that my personality type craves newness. I love change. Initially, I thought learning this would help me understand myself and help me to work to my preferences but it reinforced my thinking that habits are more difficult for me than the rest of the human race.

It was only when I started to focus on my thoughts that I realised that my patterns of thinking were habits too. My thoughts that habits won't work for me, I like things to be different, I suck at habits, were in fact all habits. Habitual thought patterns weren't helping me get where I wanted to be and even though I knew it intellectually, that if you change your thoughts, you can change your life, I wasn't acting on this knowledge. I started to monitor my thoughts.

When I recognised the old thought of 'I suck at habits' I would remind myself that I had mastered plenty of productivity habits that had changed my life. I had started to use my calendar to organise my days and weeks, I used a task manager and I practised the inbox zero technique like a pro. All of these were habits that had helped me from feeling out of control and chaotic to having more success with my business and helping me write my first book. It was the habit of meditation, exercise and rising early that I wanted to bring into my life that had seriously challenged my ability to change.

I eventually mastered these habits... and it began with rising early. I must admit straight away that It took many years of trial and error, adjustments in other habits such as earlier bedtimes and saying goodbye to late night movies, but the real change eventually came when I took control of my thoughts. Once I recognised how my inner dialogue was damaging my potential, I set about taking control of it. I did it by jumping out of bed before the negative talk began. And this is how I started to rise before my bull. With rising early I made space for the first habit I wanted to create... meditation. Once I mastered this habit, it was easier to stack the habit of exercise on top of my existing habit and a chain of habits were initiated that have helped me to achieve great things, things that my lazy rebellious former self would never have believed possible.

Over time I started to see that my days were made up of a sum of my habits. The days I exercised and meditated were always positive days. The days I went to bed late, skipped my morning routine tended to be not so successful. My happiness each day had a direct correlation with how I overcame my internal resistance by doing what I wanted. How much control I had over my day was determined by my morning routine.

This book will seek to explain how habits are formed and how we can both make and break them. With a better understanding of the nature of habits and how the brain creates them, you will be able to nurture the positive habits that will bring you closer to true happiness.

Aside from its cuteness, the Axolotl takes regeneration to the next level

2

Mimicking The Salamander

THE salamander, despite its lizard-like appearance, is in fact an amphibian. You may have known this but did you know salamanders come in many coloured varieties, stripes, spots and dots and range in size from an inch to six feet? Did you know that amongst the many varieties of salamander, one trait they commonly hold is that they have the ability to regenerate entire limbs or parts of their organs?

The Axolotl is the salamander that interests me the most, the Axolotl also known as the Mexican walking fish, looks like it belongs in a Disney movie with a persistent smile on its chubby face. Aside from its cuteness, the Axolotl takes regeneration to the next level. As well as being able to regenerate limbs like their average cousins, Axolotl can rebuild their jaws, spines and brains. Yes, they can actually rebuild their brains!

Any type of regeneration that happens in the animal kingdom is of course done for the survival of the species. While human beings are not yet able to physically regenerate limbs and organs, we do have the ability to regenerate the content our brains. We can change our thoughts and change the chemical composition of our brains by changing our actions. This ability will not only improve our chances of survival; it will also enhance our ability to thrive. So if you want to mimic the Axolotl and recreate your brain, it's time to shed the old skin.

Choosing A New Skin

How often do you look at your circumstances and blame the

outside world for the experience you are having right now? I would be slimmer, fitter, richer but... (add) some really lame excuse?

The life you are living now is a culmination of the choices you have made. I know when I am overweight, it's because I chose pizza over salad or TV over exercise. If I have a bad day, it's probably because I chose an extra hour of sleep over meditation. Everyday we make hundreds of choices that determine the quality of our lives. We choose our actions and so too do we choose our thoughts. Both have an impact on who we are and the quality of the life we lead. Over time a lot of these thoughts and actions become automated. We tend to think the same thoughts and do the same things because it's easier that way.

If you want to change your life you need to start by understanding that change is within your control, that the new habit you seek does not lie outside your reach. When we make excuses about why we haven't changed yet and why we haven't done the things we want to do, we disempower ourselves. We are choosing to see ourselves and our lives in a certain way and what happens to us as out of our control.

Press Pause On The Old

Most of us live in the matrix type world where we fall prey to subconsciously installing the rewritten programmes of our culture and society. For most of us, our culture dictates that we must study hard, get a good job, get married and have children.

When we fail to execute this programme fully we feel inadequate and somehow flawed. It's time to rewrite the code, but we can only rewrite it when we are ready to wake up and admit that life doesn't have to follow this prewritten script. When we realise that we are in control of the programme and we have full access to change a few lines of script or do a complete re-write, we are given the keys to the kingdom. But, of course, the problem for most of us is we don't understand the code. We try to access it at times, we think we have grasped it but then our original programme reboots and wipes out our upgrade and we have to start again from scratch.

So would you like to learn a little bit more about coding? Would you like to have the power to choose how you think each day? Little by little, line by line, you can rewrite your life, gradually creating new behaviours that serve you better than the old ones and help you to live an upgraded version of the life that you choose to create.

Here's the deal; you cannot become a better person whilst staying the person you are today.

This may seem like an odd statement but it's the chief reason we fail at habit creation, goal-setting and other personal change attempts. Who you are today is not the person you want to be tomorrow and until you are willing to let your current self go, you will be climbing a hill for the rest of your life.

Maybe you want to lose weight but you don't want to stop eating greasy foods, you want to get fit but you don't want to work out, you want to feel good while continuing to drink wine every evening. Unfortunately, these pairings are incompatible, we speak about balance, a little of everything cannot be bad for you. While this may sometimes but true, it's not true when you are still not getting the results that you want. Maybe a little wine is ok but when it leads to overeating or staying up late, then drinking is not ok for someone who wants to upgrade their life.

First let's take a look at the programmes that have been installed since you were a child. These include your beliefs, your values, your emotions, your thoughts, your habits and your experiences. They all add up to make you who you are today. So if you are not happy and want to change, whether it's a big or small change your beliefs, your values, your emotions, your thoughts and your habits will all have to change to some degree. Positive change involves understanding who you currently are and what contributed to the life you live today while also deciding who you want to be tomorrow.

Are You Bringing That Suitcase?

We have adopted some untrue beliefs about who we are over the years. Fortunately your brain has the ability to change. Neuroplasticity is the capacity of the brain to change or reorganise its neural networks or behaviour in response to new information. You can learn to change your behaviors at any stage in life. Scientists have established that our brain is constantly growing and that we have the ability to learn and change at any age. Neuroplasticity research has now established that our brain is not a static cell mass, but a dynamic neural network that has the capability of significant growth. Think of how water makes channels in sand or soil, each time you practice your habit the deeper the channel gets. This holds for habitual actions, habitual thoughts or emotions. When you fail to practice, the channel doesn't dissolve immediately, we don't forget all that we know instantly so the benefit of the hard work you have done doesn't instantly disappear. This is also why your negative habitual thoughts don't disappear after a week of positive affirmations.

The way you behave is not who you are but who you have allowed yourself to become. If you want to be less reactive, more patient, calmer or more empathetic you can train your brain to help you become the person you want to become. But just as you can easily create new pathways in the brain to support who you want to become, remember that this has been happening on autopilot all your life, the person you are now is a result of all your past experiences. And all these past experiences we often refer to as baggage.

Everything you do each day, every choice you make, is influenced by the invisible baggage you carry around. Thoughts, emotions, values and beliefs are all invisible to others and often not clear to ourselves. This baggage doesn't always carry negative stuff, it carries all our positive thoughts and beliefs too, but most of it is happening to us out of sight.

So a lot of who you are is subconsciously memorised, habitual thoughts and habitual behaviours reinforcing each other even though they may not be good for us. The body prefers what is familiar to what is different and if sitting on the sofa is more familiar than going for a walk by the sea, then you can be sure that this is the behaviour your butt is routing for.

How many times have you logically decided change is necessary, commit to it and fail? Too often I would guess. This is because humans naturally resist the uncertain. Our brain is more comfortable with how things currently are and will resist any change. For this reason we need to create more certainty for our brain when we try to change. The more we plan a change and have clear sight of what it involves, the less our brain will resist it. In the next part of the book you will find out more about how to plan and design your new habit, but first we need to tackle what's going on inside.

How we think, how we feel and how we act add up to who we are. So to move your life in a certain direction all three of these areas should be in alignment to create momentum.

Think

The thoughts that we think impact how we feel. These are influenced by the invisible baggage and the experiences we have each day. Our thoughts are also affected by our emotions which may or may not have been triggered by a thought.

Feel

Our emotions are influenced by our thoughts and our actions. If we go for a physical run, the endorphins from that run will modify our chemical composition and impact how we feel. If we practice acts of kindness this will affect how we feel. If we think happy thoughts or thoughts of gratitude, this too can make us feel good.

Act

Our daily actions or behaviours are influenced by how we feel and the thoughts that we are having. These actions or habits can also positively or negatively change our thoughts and our feelings

So you can see that how we think, feel and act are all interconnected and mutually significant.

We know our thoughts are powerful and can impact our physical reality. A simple thought about a person you are attracted too can create a physical arousal in your body. The thought of a juicy lemon creates a physical reaction in your salivary glands and a stressful thought of something that worries you can create a feeling of anxiety to the level of a panic. So the loop between our thoughts and our feelings is ongoing. We feel good, we think nice thoughts which makes us feel good and continue to think nice

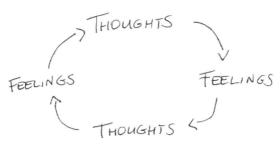

thoughts. On the flip side your partner leaves you, you feel lousy, you think disempowering and fear based thoughts about the future, reinforcing the sad emotions you are feeling.

So if you think about your partner leaving you, you feel like crap, and your therapist tells you to think positive, think happy thoughts and you will feel amazing yes?

No, while trying to think positive will have some influence on your mood and your emotions, it won't be enough to shift you into a positive mood straight away.

But if we include our actions into the loop, let's say we go to a dance class, we meet up with friends that make us laugh or watch a comedy, these actions will physically shift your emotions and along with the positive thoughts of "I can be happy alone" or "I will meet someone who loves respects me," we can move towards feeling better more quickly.

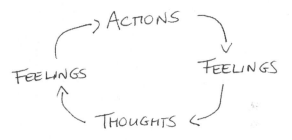

Imagine the following scenario — you wake up late, fail to exercise and arrive to your meeting late and you receive a lot of work to be done for tomorrow. The results of waking late may contribute to a feeling of stress and you may think negative thoughts about how you have failed yourself again. On the flipside you wake up early, exercise and meditate and feel great and empowered, arrive to work early have time to prepare for the meeting and when work is thrown your way you know how to push back.

Your actions (waking up late or early) will contribute to you having negative or positive thoughts about yourself and your emotions of stress and satisfaction. So our actions play a large part in how we think and how we feel also.

Building The Happiness Wall

While focusing on the positive is a strategy that will help you move towards a happier life, if you were to only focus on positive and happy thoughts you wouldn't get the required long term effect we all want when we want to change our lives. It is more difficult for your thoughts alone to impact the big picture.

Think of your happiness as a wall and your thoughts as pebbles, every positive thought is going to make a positive impression and help you build that wall of happiness but the wall with be small and it will take a long time to get the result you desire. A wall built of pebbles will have more potential to break apart. As every positive thought won't necessarily make it to being a positive feeling.

Whereas if you think of feelings as rocks, when you directly impact the feeling, you are contributing more to your happiness wall.

THOUGHTS   FEELINGS   THE HAPPINESS WALL

When you think positive thoughts and do the things that directly impact your feelings you are more likely to build a stronger and longer lasting wall of happiness.

What directly impacts our feelings?

There are many activities that can and will improve how you feel. They can be grouped into the following areas –
* Physical Activities, such as exercise and walks in nature
* Mental Activities, such as meditation and mindfulness
* Acts of Charity, helping those in need
* Practice of Gratitude, giving thanks for everything you have in life.

Physical Activity

There is an abundance of studies on how physical activity positively impacts our health, wellbeing and mood. Regular walks, running, going to the gym will all help to raise your endorphin levels and make you feel more confident, happier and less stressed. Team sports can be a great way to get active and social at the same time. Dancing is another great way to raise your spirits even in a period of darkness. Whether it's at a nightclub or at home in your sitting room, it's a super way to get moving and impact how you feel at the same time.

Mental Activities

Meditation and Mindfulness — no longer just for monks and gurus — are becoming part of the western world. The research suggests that meditation sharpens skills like attention, memory and emotional intelligence. Other studies have shown meditation to help reduce stress and positively impact resilience. Meditation, like exercise, has a multitude of benefits for both your personal and professional life while having the ability to directly alter the way you feel. Other activities like conversation, or puzzles all distract the thinking mind and can help you to live more in the moment and not allow negative thoughts to negatively impact your feelings.

Acts of Charity

Being the mother of teenagers, I attended a seminar by an Irish psychologist by the name of Enda Murphy. While I picked up several good nuggets of advice on the teenage brain and positive parenting of adolescents one point he made really stuck with me. Here is my interpretation. Teenagers are narcissistic... the world revolves around them which can lead to self-pity and sometimes depression. The psychologist mentioned that he'd never treated an adolescent for depression or anxiety who was involved in a charity or community project. When teenagers see that the world is bigger than themselves, when they understand they are part of something bigger, they rarely suffer from depression. Fortunately adults know acts of charity and kindness will warm the heart and create a feeling of well-being.

Gratitude

The practice of gratitude has also been the subject of many scientific studies in recent years. Gratitude helps us to look at what is right about our lives. To focus on what we have rather than what we don't have. It's almost impossible to feel low or depressed while feeling grateful. If you practice a daily ritual of gratitude it will improve well-being and helps you to feel good about your live.

These examples of activities will all contribute to positive emotions. Helping add to the rocks on your happiness wall. So if you can include any of these activities in your life you have a greater chance of feeling good more often. When you feel good, your thoughts will be more positive and empowering.

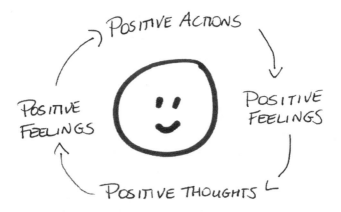

The River Of Change

Here's the challenge; the challenge as a human being is to continuously do the things that you know make you happy and contribute to your inner and outer success. Creating habits isn't easy but it's the key to long-term happiness and positive emotion. Habit helps you to get out of your thinking mind, knowing what you should be doing and into your subconscious mind. Your subconscious mind is a storehouse of stimulus-response recordings, some come from instinct and others learned experiences. We want to tap into this programme that runs automatically and use it to help you to carry out the positive actions that make you a better person. Habit reduces the need for thought to carry out a command.

Here's the reality:

Typical internal conversation:
Thought = *Time to exercise*
Another thought = *Don't need to do it right away*
Another thought = *I'll have more time later*
Later Thought = *I'm tired now, maybe I'll leave it until tomorrow*

When we create lasting habits we stop having conversations like the one above. Habit bypasses thought and encourages less interference in the primary plan. When we create a new habit whether it's a positive habit or a negative habit, you will find that there is less and less conversation happening in your head. You start from the pre-programmed plan and action starts to happen without too much interference.

Before we get to this stage, you will have the most bizarre conversations with yourself that might be embarrassing to say aloud. The reason for this is that your habitual thoughts and feelings are so engrained in who you are, the same actions create the same neurology. For years you have been having the same thoughts and those thoughts have created the same feelings. The chemical connection between the thought and feeling is something your body is very used to. So when you try to change that, your body reacts negatively! Hey dude, where's my fix? The body become addicted to the same feelings, even if those feelings are not wonderful positive ones. If it is the one you are familiar with, then you will crave it. I believe this is why some people appear to be addicted to negativity and emotional drama. The familiarity is more important to them than whether it is a positive or negative feeling.

When we step away from what's familiar, it's like walking into the River of Change. The old-self riverbank is in need of an upgrade but its familiar. The "new-self riverbank" looks attractive, it's exactly where you want to be but it requires stepping into the River of Change. The river looks ok to start with, it's exciting, it's different but then the water starts to flow in different directions and it feels a little different than you expected. It becomes more unfamiliar. You like the familiar. Your brain likes the familiar, so rather than keep wading out to get to the other side, what do you do? You jump back out and you feel safe. You may dip your toe in again but not today or tomorrow. Let's just settle back into the familiar self and play it safe for a while.

This is what typically happens each time we attempt to change. Every new year we jump head on into that river and we start to wade in. This year I'll do it. This year will be different but it's not and the reason it's not is because you are still carrying the same baggage. It doesn't matter if you get new luggage, this year you might try a rucksack or a duffle bag but if you have the same old pants inside you won't get comfortably to the other side. You may do what I did for years, struggle and fight to reach the other side, celebrate for a bit and then jump back quickly because I didn't belong on the other side.

In the next chapter we will take a look at what's inside that luggage and if we can upgrade it, we can take on the steps to create new habits for good.

For much of life we waste our precious time blending in, living the life of least resistance

3

The Owl In The Tree

HAVE you ever stood still like a tree? If you can't remember doing it, I bet you did it in junior school, standing still as you imagine you are the mighty oak creating shelter for all the woodland creatures. The mighty trees in the woodlands of the Florida coast provide shelter for a host of woodland animals. The Eastern Screech owl is one of them. Like all owls, it emerges from its nest at dusk to hunt small birds and rodents. The owl is heard more than it is seen, as its name implies, because the feathers of an adult screech owl blend in perfectly with the bark and wood of the trees in the area where it lives. This camouflage helps protect it and its young from predators. Like many prey animals, they use camouflage to allow them to blend in with certain aspects of their environment. This increases the animals' chance of survival.

Problem with a lot of humans is that they stood still like a tree back in playschool and they still want to play that game. They want to blend into their surroundings, sink into the sofa where no one will see them. Hide in bed until their young drag them out. For much of life we waste our precious time blending in, living the life of least resistance. Stay small, stay safe and don't move away from your tree pose. The beliefs that we have formed over the years have limited our potential to live rich and fulfilling lives. Standing still and letting life pass you by unnoticed might be the wise move for a Screech Owl but not for a human being full of potential.

Uncovering The Essence

What are your guiding principles? What do you believe to be true about yourself or about the world you live in? Your beliefs provide direction and meaning in life, they are the filters to your world. Beliefs are formed according to the culture you grow up in, the environment within that culture and the experiences and exposure you have had throughout your life. We often think that beliefs are static but that is not that case. Beliefs are a choice and they can be changed. High performers choose their beliefs; they choose to believe they can surpass pre-conceived limits. Practicing high performing habits imprint positive neural pathways that reinforce what they already know. Electrical impulses encourage them in the direction of greatness. They know that playing it safe is not an option, because playing it safe doesn't get the results.

Recovering alcoholics follow the 12-step programme to recovery. The programme encourages them to go to a meeting every day. The aim is to create a powerful habit, reinforcing the support and positive environment that they are in need of. Unfortunately, the statistics show that not all succeed. The majority of addicts who succeed in overcoming addiction are not necessarily the ones attending daily meeting but those that find a belief in a higher power. In the lowest moments, perhaps an addict doesn't have sufficient inner belief to overcome addiction but if they believe they have someone looking out for them, maybe that's what helps them through.

The 12-step programme gives hope, a belief that life can get better and that you can and will succeed. Where can we find this belief when it is not currently there? How can we find the faith to persevere and behave like the people we admire?

Let's take a look at your current beliefs? The things you believe about yourself and about the world will determine your future possibilities and the level of success you deem to be possible in the future. What we want to do is to uncover your conscious and unconscious beliefs about who you are and what your potential and abilities are. It's the subconscious beliefs that effectively run our lives. You need both the conscious and subconscious mind working in unison if you want to change your world.

Take some time to answer the following questions below or in the *Rise Before Your Bull* workbook

What are the things your parents told you as a child?

_____

_____

What are the things your teachers said?

_____

_____

What does your culture say about success?

_____

_____

What are your current beliefs about money?

_____

_____

What are your current beliefs about your health?

_____

_____

How successful do you think you can become?

_____

_____

Think of a habit you have tried to create and failed. What are the beliefs you have around that habit and why you have failed? Write them down here.

_____

_____

The more honest you are with yourself and answering these questions, the more likely you are to overcome any barriers you have had in the past and move forward to create all the long-lasting habits that will change your life for the better.

Please re-read that last paragraph. Do you believe what you have just read? If you do not believe that last paragraph, ask yourself why? Do not read on until you have figured it out.

Bringing your limiting beliefs to the light will help you to critically assess if they are actually true and if you want to keep them. If a belief isn't serving you, why not change it? For example, if you believe that you cannot relax without smoking a cigarette, this is a belief that needs to be challenged and then reprogrammed. You may use hypnosis or simple affirmations but it is important to reinsert a positive belief to challenge the negative one. According to a study carried out by Szegedy-Maszak in 2005, the subconscious mind is running the show 95 per cent of the time, so uncovering what's going on in there is a priority.

If you have uncovered the belief that you think is holding you back, how can you re-programme this belief? It maybe something like "I never finish anything" or I've tried so many times before it's not going to work this time?" Start by challenging the belief, for example "I never finish anything." Is this really true? List the things you have finished in your life, by doing this you are proving to yourself this belief is not a fact and is untrue. Now every time you consciously think this thought you remind yourself that it is untrue and that you have finished many things in the past. Every time you think of starting a new habit that may have been hindered by this limiting belief, remind yourself and speak to yourself in a more positive manner. You are getting better at finishing things. Keep up the good work.

What Do You Value?

Knowing who you are and how you want to live your life each day will equip you with the toolkit required to create that new life. When you are living outside your values, you are pulling when you should be pushing.

What do you believe is important in the way that you live your life and carry out your work?

Your values are what help you to figure out your priorities, and understanding your priorities is crucial to be able to live your best life. When you are clear about your values, it's easier to decide if the goals you are working towards are your right goals. Living contra to your values is an uncomfortable place to be and not a long-term strategy for happiness.

Take the time to work out what your true values are. Start by writing a list of all the values that you think are important, honesty, hard work, harmony, enjoyment, achievement.... Write down all the values that resonate with you. (In Appendix B on Page 161 you will find a list of values to prompt you). This exercise will create clarity around your purpose in life and what you want your future life to look like. Don't waste precious time being unsure.

After choosing all the values you think are important, whittle down the ones you've chosen by comparing each one to the next. Ask yourself which ones hold more importance for you? Try to create a priority list, identifying your top values. Get to a point where you can clearly recognise your most important value or at least your top three.

If you identify that one of your core values is achievement but you haven't achieved anything of great value for the past 10 years, it is safe to assume you haven't be functioning at your best.

Satisfying your values is core to your inner happiness. Without this, will power, mental strength and resilience will have a bigger battle on their hands. Understanding your values and living a life that is true to them will contribute to your personal confidence and obviously to your success.

Who Is Boss Around Here?

Of the thousands of thoughts you have each day, how many of these do you think are friendly? Are your thoughts supporting you and uplifting you or do they drag you down? Spend some time monitoring your thoughts. You may be surprised to find that there is a lot of negativity directed your way. The internal dialogue that plays daily is not as positive and supportive as it should be. Is your inner voice like a cranky aunt who is never happy with her lot? Maybe she spends her day commenting on the fact that you put on a couple of pounds since Christmas or that your cooking isn't as good as your mother's. Does she tell you all the things you should be but aren't? Ignore the aunt take control of your thoughts as well as your life.

Here's something startling to remember — the dialogue that goes on is your head is actually within your control. You are the boss and you can stop it anytime. The rules are very simple; No more negative self-deprecating thoughts. You will now replace them with positive supportive and encouraging thoughts.

"I think, therefore I am" An interpretation of the Descartes philosophy is the belief that our thinking is who we are. If thinking proves our existence what determines the quality of that existence? Could the quality of your thoughts determine what you can become? If so your ability to control those thoughts would determine your happiness and success.

It's crucial to understand that you are more than your current thoughts. A lot of your thinking comes from habitual thoughts some stemming from childhood. Your past thinking has led you to where you are today but that can change.

Hypnosis, cognitive behavioural therapy, meditation, NLP are all methods that can help us control the thoughts in our head and manipulate them to our advantage. We must learn to train our brains to produce only the thoughts that serve us, that nurture us and support us in our quest for a better world.

There are many methods available today to help us replace negative thoughts and replace them with more positive and productive ones. Simple strategies to help you by firstly becoming aware of your thinking patterns and then trying to change them. Of course if your negative thoughts are causing you deep anxiety or depression, please seek out professional help. But if your negative thoughts are preventing you from running a race, writing a book or starting a new business, then you can take it upon yourself to change them.

By recognising the harmful negative thought patterns and replacing them with positive uplifting thoughts you will experience a giant leap towards creating the life you want.

Monitor your thoughts for a day, become the observer of your mind. Watch and note how often you have a negative thought. Tell yourself to STOP every time you observe a negative thought. Better still, order yourself to STOP.

Ask yourself if the thought is serving you in any way. Remember that not all negative thoughts are harmful or useless, there are times where they will help you remove yourself from danger or help you come up with better results and solutions to problems. Generally we know that positive thoughts are more empowering and beneficial for our personal advancement and growth, especially when they are replacing negative thoughts about yourself.

If you are over 40 you may be noticing that your body doesn't work like it used to. Your knees hurt, your back aches in the mornings and you worry every time someone asks you to lift something heavy. When you allow these thoughts to take over, it is safe to assume you probably would never consider running a marathon or climbing a mountain.

Straight away you can change the thoughts to remind yourself about all the bits that do work. You have two strong legs, two strong arms, eyes that see perfectly, ears that hear perfectly. The doctor told you you had the heart of a horse and your lungs are fresh as a daisy. If you took some cod liver oil for your knees and joined a group of like-minded people all planning to run a marathon, you probably could do it.

Which Emotions Do You Choose?

What are the emotions that you tend to carry around? Is love an emotion people relate to you? Does fear dictate everything you do? What about self-pity? Regret? Confidence, what emotions dictate your days?

Previously I mentioned about how powerful our emotions can be, sometimes triggering physical responses in the body. Chemicals such as adrenaline are secreted into the blood stream when we feel anxious or nervous. These reactions can eventually be craved by the body; you can become the adrenaline junkie whose life isn't worth living unless it means living on the edge.

Emotions such as anger which appear to be very reactive and not thought based, are still rooted to the way we think about things. Anger is triggered in the brain when we perceive something that causes us discomfort or unease. Neurotransmitter chemicals called catecholamines are released causing a burst of energy. The amygdala is the part of the brain responsible for identifying threats to our well-being. It recognises threats before our cortex sees them and rationalises the level of threat. But it is possible to control our response mechanism and also to learn strategies to keep our reactions in check.

If we can first become aware of what triggers our emotions, we can change the way we think about things and react accordingly. Sometimes our triggers come from painful memories of childhood which may not be conscious. Other times, someone might make us feel inferior with a nasty comment which may trigger the same emotion as an adult. There are occasions when we react irrationally to comments people make which don't make sense to us logically, we know it shouldn't elicit such a strong emotional reaction... but it does.

Understanding your emotional triggers will help you to identify the emotions you carry around that aren't helping you.

What are your emotional triggers? How do you react to the following?

When someone rejects you?

_____

_____

When you are blamed for something?

_____

_____

When someone is critical towards you?

_____

_____

When someone doesn't listen to you?

_____

_____

When someone is very needy?

_____

_____

You may have a number of these triggers or you may have completely different ones but when you understand what triggers your dominant emotions, you will gradually be able to move forward. Again if you have suffered from emotional or physical abuse, I suggest you contact a professional to help you work through your emotional triggers.

Once you have figured out what baggage you are carrying, you can start to understand where your current thoughts, beliefs and emotions come from. Do you need to bring the baggage to the other side of the river? Can you let go of the beliefs that don't serve you and weigh you down by choosing a lighter load with more positive beliefs? The choice is always yours.

PART 2

The Habit Method

The greater your awareness, the more empowered you will be

4

The Lion,
The Llama
And The Lizard

THE lion, the king of the jungle has been the subject of man's intent to tame, train and change for many years. Initially these attempts were mostly for our own entertainment, where these beautiful animals were degraded and humiliated in what was meant to be the show of the century. In more recent years, the desire to train these and other wild animals is for conservation reasons and more often than not for the animal's own health and safety.

The first attempts at training a lion in the early 1800s were a gradual effort at earning the animal's trust, later lion trainers used physical violence and scare tactics to force the lion into doing what man wanted. Today most animal trainers use a theory called 'operant conditioning', a fundamental concept in behavioral psychology accredited to psychologist B. F. Skinner. Skinner said that behaviour which is reinforced tends to be repeated or strengthened and behaviour which is not reinforced tends to die out or be weakened. Skinner originally carried out research on mice to test his assumptions.

Many years later animal trainers use 'operant conditioning' to teach animals to connect a behaviour with a cue and then they reward the animal for correct behavior. Whenever the animal behaves in the right way, the trainer offers positive reinforcement, usually in the form of food.

But lions are not the only animals to respond to a cue and a reward. The llama, believe it or not, can be trained to do a bunch of things. Archaeological findings show that llamas were living with man back in 3000 BC. The Inca empire used llamas in many ways. They carried the load, their wool kept them warm and unfortunately for the llamas they also played a role in the religious and ceremonial life of the Incas, and were often sacrificed to the gods.

Llamas are still highly regarded in South America where an estimated 7,000,000 of them are located. They were introduced to the USA in the early 1900s and their numbers remain in the high thousands. In more recent years, llamas have had their fashion moment, the object of adornment on everything from jumpers to shower curtains. They overtook the flamingos and the unicorns to have their personal moment of glory. While the public image was being raised by the fashion industry, they didn't point out that llamas have a nasty habit, one that most trainers attempt to break in them. Llamas are spitters. Yes, that cute woolly creature will spit right in your face if he doesn't like the cut of your gib. Apparently they do it with other llamas when they are irritated and just because they have been domesticated and live with humans, we shouldn't expect to be treated any differently. The same behavioural technique is used successfully on llama to eliminate their dirty spitting habit.

And then we come to the lizards; Blue and Cooper were a couple of endangered Iguanas at Audubon Nature Institute in New Orleans. Not only were they a couple of endangered Iguanas but the intention was that they become a couple, romantic style.

One of the things that Blue and Coopers handlers needed to do was ensure that their treasured pair weren't suffering from stress. Being a critically endangered species, stress is not good. When reptiles are stressed, they release stress hormones into their blood stream which can cause both physical and mental problems. All sorts of things can stress reptiles from differences in temperature or humidity or simply the confinement of captivity. Continuous high levels of stress hormones can inhibit reproduction just like in humans and also suppress the reptiles' immune system making them more vulnerable to disease and even death. Obviously stress needs to be avoided at all costs.

Blue, the male, could be aggressive at feeding time and it was important that Cooper, his mate felt safe around him in order to be able to eat her meals without being challenged or intimidated by him.

Blue and Cooper's trainers taught them how to be calm at feeding time. By using clicker training. They taught them how to "station" and "wait" and by doing this they were able to eliminate Blue's aggressive behaviour and make Cooper feel at ease. The training meant that the Iguanas became a healthy and happy breeding pair.

Clicker training is when a mechanical device that makes a short click is used to tell an animal when they are doing the right thing. The clicker clearly indicates to the animal that desired behaviour and a reward is given for positive reinforcement.

Clicker training has been deemed to be so successful in animal training it is often used in sports training where verbal reinforcement can sometimes become confusing for the athlete. When an athlete repeats an action it is easy for the trainer to click when the exact movement or behaviour is seen, helping the athlete to perfect their technique much more quickly than with a verbal response. Verbal response can also be interpreted badly as tone can be picked up from the coach whether rightly or wrongly and this can affect the self-belief and efficacy of the positive reinforcement. When you hear 'Good Job,' it can mean a host of things where a click in response to a movement only has one meaning.

So clicker training can be used to condition animals and humans alike but I am suggesting a less intrusive approach for you, one that allows you to understand and leverage behavioural psychology along with other practical steps to help you to create new long lasting habits.

Over my many years trying and failing and trying again and watching my clients do the same, I've learnt what works and what doesn't. Below is the model I have used to master the habits of meditation, exercise, healthy eating, writing, staying organised and believe it not keeping my bedroom tidy (the last one being the most difficult for me).

In the last chapter, we focused on the limiting beliefs that may have prevented us from successfully creating habits in the past. It's important that this step is carried out to allow space for the positive habit creation to begin. So if you haven't actually answered the questions in Chapter Three, please go back and do that now before you continue with this chapter. This chapter explains the component parts and encourages you to take action towards creating the habits that will give you the life that you want.

The Habit Method

Breaking down the component parts helps to ensure we have all angles covered when attempting to create a new habit. You may recognise instantly which component part has been missing in your previous attempts or you may see that each one of them needs work, but don't fret, the greater your awareness, the more empowered you will be to put the individual parts in place so that this time there will be no stopping you.

Each part is as important as the next and each one must be considered if you are to create a habit that will stand by you till you are in your nineties. That is, of course, if the habits that you are currently creating are the ones you still want later in life. You may choose to keep up the knitting and you never know, if you maintain the energy levels that you will get from doing daily exercise, you might still be doing Kick flips and Ollies too.

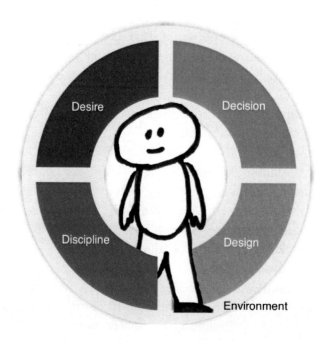

Desire: The first and possibly the most important component of habit creation is desire. You must have a burning need to create the new habit and understand why you want it. What is the goal that you long to reach and why is it so important in your life? Without true desire you will be weak when the going gets tough. Your desire is what will fuel the fire when the light is burning low.

Decision: Making the decision to move forward will carry your desire from thought towards action. When you decide that you are going to do something you must make a commitment. Move away from half-hearted decisions and promise yourself that you are going to do what it takes in order to get the goals that you want. Having clarity around what you want and making sure that it's your priority right now will propel you forward towards success.

Design: Once you know what you want and you have committed to getting it you need to make a plan. Spending time in advance to get clear about the how, where, what and when will leave less chances for opting out. How are you going to achieve this? What do you need to get going? Who will support you? Thinking through the plan in advance and having tools and techniques will help you move into action.

Discipline: Although we now know that habit formation is not just about willpower and discipline, the latter always plays an important role. When you make your commitment, you must have the discipline to follow through. Until your habit becomes second nature, it will be necessary to rely on discipline to help you establish the new routines. Once the habit has been formed there will still be days and times when you don't feel like it or you are too busy. There will also be times when you are sick and fall out of the habit.

Environment: Often we fail to acknowledge the role the environment plays in creating a habit. It influences our state of mind and our state of being. Some environments will be harsher than others and your habit will need to be created accordingly. A challenging environment is not an excuse to opt out or to give up, a challenging environment needs more planning and adaptation. A little bit more creative design and discipline may be required to ensure your actions lead you to success.

With each part of the model there is a different component at play.

When you focus on desire and are clear about what it is you want and why, your thoughts and beliefs have to be in alignment in order to support you in moving forward towards your goals. Do you currently belief you have the ability to achieve your goal or to create this new habit? Are the thoughts you are thinking each day supportive and encouraging towards getting the goal? Your daily thoughts are going to be the support system for your desire. Your thoughts must encourage and propel you forward towards creating your new habit.

The decision to take action is an important one and one that should not be taken too lightly. Often we get confused about which direction to take and what to do next. Taking time to consider the possibilities and identify your priorities will help you to make a decision that you are confident in and ensure that the direction that you choose is the right one for you in your life right now. Once the decision is made your thoughts can once again support you in taking the steps forward.

Habit design is an important step in the process and one that will stand to you. The more effort and thought put into this part of the process ensures that when you take action, it will be the right sort and in a manner that suits your circumstances. Your design will answer all of the questions you have about how, when and where the action is going to take place. Leaving these questions unanswered is always a recipe for failure when it comes to habit formation.

For discipline to work it requires strong command of your thoughts. When you allow runaway negative or unsupportive thoughts to hijack your brain, discipline usually takes a back seat. To master the slippery art of self-discipline, you will need to continue to think positive, empowering and supportive thoughts while you commit to continuously take action.

When the environment is designed optimally it will be easier to take the regular action required to create your new habits. Make sure you have what you need to get to you your goals. Take daily action to ensure your environment is supporting you and not sabotaging you.

To help you create your new habits I have designed the Habit Canvas (which you will find on Page 160). You can fill in the Canvas as you work through each area of The Habit Method.

The desire to change is the ember that will keep the fires burning when the rain comes and believe me the rain will come... of that you can be sure

5

Desire to Change

MISTAKENLY, we occasionally think that our inability to get what we want from life is down to our deficient willpower. We just can't seem to muster enough of it to persist with the changes we need to make. From reading the previous chapters you will be aware that creating lasting habits is not merely a question of willpower as one of several other factors could be preventing your success. Lack of belief, conflicting values or perhaps lack of a plan but the one thing that is essential before you waste time with all the other stuff is desire. The desire to change is the ember that will keep the fires burning when the rain comes and believe me the rain will come... of that you can be sure.

"Desire is the starting point of all achievement, not a hope, not a wish, but a keen pulsating desire which transcends everything" — Napoleon Hill.

Desire is a longing for something or wanting something to happen, but desire needs to run deep. The greater your desire, the greater your chances. If the desire is not there, can you create it? Possibly, but it's more about fanning the embers and removing the ash than creating it from nothing.

Are you focusing on the right things? We have a preconceived notion about what we need to do to get what we want. We are often wrong. We say we want more money, bigger cars and houses. How about focusing on how you want to feel? Maybe what you really want is happiness, joy, freedom, security and love? Think about the emotions you want in life and let them be your guide when setting your goals and thinking about why?

Connecting With 'The Why'

I once visited a personal trainer who had expertise in the area of hips. I had been suffering for many years with a pain at the top of my right leg. Doctors and X-rays showed nothing, personal trainers, physiotherapists, osteopaths and many more alternative therapists had their differing views on what ailed me. It ranged from tight hip flexors to rigid vertebrae to stored hurt in my heart. Two tennis-less years later, I finally got an MRI which showed minor damage to my hip, nothing too serious to merit doing anything about it. My pain ranges from a 1-to-8 but is inconsistent. In those two years I'd stopped doing regular exercise following the plan of each therapist I visited. I'd hope they would give me a solution. Instead I started to put on weight, to become more inflexible and unfit. Then I met a gym owner who was confident he knew how to get my strength back and hopefully delay the possibility of hip surgery.

I visited him at his gym where he brought me to his office, I had bought new gym gear for the occasion. He took out a pen and paper and asked me many, many questions. Thorough I thought. Then the questions got deeper, what do I value in life? I was getting a little frustrated and reminded him I was here for him to fix my hip not solve my life's problems. He told me that I had been outsourcing my health and if I wanted to make a difference to my health I needed to take responsibility for my own health. It stung a little but he was right. I probably had been waiting for someone else to fix me and had spent quite a lot of money in search of the right person to do that. So point taken.

He continued with my values, what did I value, my family, my work and my health? But obviously not my health, if I hadn't worked out in a year... ok, ok good point. What had I spent the majority of my money on in the last year? My family and my business, what percentage on each? Eh, growing myself and the business gets quite a lot. Is he implying my work is more important than my kids? I'll let it pass. More questions, more frustrated answers. More truths that I may or may not have needed to learn from my gym instructor. Until finally we got to where he wanted to go.

As a professional speaker, how good do you think you will look hobbling onto a stage? What about crutches? Well, if I need an operation I'll have to have an operation. Did I know how long the recovery was and how much time I'd have to take off work? I had some idea. So if I have to take time off work, could I survive without working? Possibly, I don't know. Maybe. Why are you asking me all this? Because you need to understand if you don't do something about your health now, you will be damaging your career, your income source and your potential to support your family.

Ouch!

So an hour later, I left the gym feeling deflated, confused and offended with unused gym gear. I couldn't understand why he spent so much time shaming me and making me feel bad about myself. Wasn't his job to help me reach my potential, feel inspired to change?

It took a while before it hits me... he was trying to give me a "why". He wanted me to understand what my desire was linked to so that in my low moments, when I lacked discipline, willpower or maybe energy, I would think of my 'why.' The only flaw in his system was the way he pushed his why onto me.

Motivation comes from either an internal or external source and that source can be either positive or negative. So fearing an outcome would be a negative source of motivation. I was not motivated by fear. My motivation comes from moving towards something positive, both internal and external. I usually have a deep internal desire to achieve something coupled with the bright lights of external rewards. I am more likely to move towards what I like rather than run from what I don't like. My personal trainer was onto something but he jumped to conclusions too soon and didn't find my why, only his.

What is your 'Why?'

Why do you want the goals that you have set? If you want to meditate... why? Saying that you have heard it's good for you isn't good enough. Personally I knew meditation was the next step in my personal evolution. I kept saying to myself if only I could create this habit, my life would change, and it did. When you connect with your 'why,' it can be just what you need to fan the flames of desire.

Think about the first habit you want to create and your why, answer the following questions if I master this habit:

How will it make me feel?

_____

_____

How will it change the thoughts I have about myself?

_____

_____

How it will change my beliefs?

_____

_____

Why do you want to create this habit in your life?

_____

_____

What Are You Willing To Cast Off?

Desire needs to be strong enough for you to let go of some of the things in your life. Although you may have a great desire for a bikini body, you will never have one if you aren't ready to let go of your regular takeaways. That six pack will forever be beyond your reach if daily beer is your way to relax. Intelligent people repeatedly fall into the trap of believing they can get their goals without changing their current reality. It's not about suffering to get what you want – it's about understanding that continuing with one habit will consistently sabotage your desire. Are you ready to let go of what's blocking your desire? Remember, that you may be holding on to the old habit because you are addicted to an old feeling, a misguided thought. "I need this beer to relax" or "I can't have fun without alcohol." You need to challenge these beliefs that are delaying your goals from manifesting.

Make sure that you don't fall for the typical mistakes, and set goals for the wrong reasons.

Because Everyone Else Does It

If all your friends have joined the gym, that doesn't mean you have to. It could, of course, be a good idea but make sure it is what you want, suits your life and it is helping you to reach your goal. Going to the gym may not be your priority right now, while exercise should always be a priority in all our lives, it doesn't have to be the gym. I have found it much easier to exercise in the comfort of my own home first thing in the morning. There was a time when I thought I should join the gym in order to push myself harder but all that did was challenge my discipline every day. I found it much more difficult to get into the car and drive to the gym than fall out of bed and onto my bike. Rather than go to the gym I needed to find a workout that pushed me physically beyond what I had been doing.

Because You Think You Should

When you start to do something because you think you probably should, the commitment won't last. Your 'why' won't be strong enough when the going gets tough. I should exercise, I should eat healthy foods, I should stop smoking. Again while all of these goals are positive, you need to connect with why you want them personally in order for the new habits created to have longevity.

Because Your Spouse/Friend Told You

How many people have given up smoking because their other half pestered them into it? We all know how that ends. If the motivation is not intrinsic, if you are doing something because someone else told you that you should, you are unlikely to succeed. Make sure every goal or new habit you try is because you want to do it, not because someone else wants you to.

There are countless other reasons why we do things that we don't truly have the internal desire for, just be sure to uncover yours.

Focusing on habits that you are motivated to move towards is going make creating those habits a lot easier than trying to form one out of duty or supposed necessity. Be clear about your desire because if you are, the next step becomes easier... the decision.

Before you move on to make the decision, what do you have a burning desire to change?

What Is Your Goal And Why Do You Want It?

_____

_____

Transfer your answer to your **Habit Canvas** on Page 160, what habit are you going to commit to?

6

The Decision To Change

TO have the burning desire to change, you have to know why you want to change and then you have to make that decision to change. Believe it or not, this is the bit that is often left out. You might know what you want, make a few half-ass attempts at getting it but you don't make the conclusive decision to move towards getting it. Sometimes this is down to fear of failure, sometimes it is because you don't have enough clarity and other times it's because life is overwhelming and you can't focus on a thought long enough to know what to do with it.

It's All About Commitment

The foundation of marriage is based on commitment. You commit to another person to stand by them no matter what, through thick and thin, in sickness and health etc. The difference between couples who live together long-term and couples who marry is a legally-binding contract, not only have you promised the other person to stay with them, now you have gone and vowed to do it, probably in front of God and country.

For some people it's easier to sign your life away to another human being till the end of time than to commit to doing exercise three times a week. We are scared to commit in case we fail. Did you know that over 60 per cent of marriages end in divorce? Odds aren't that good are they? but people take the risk every day because they believe the rewards are greater than the risk. If you commit to going to the gym, or running or playing basketball or football or dancing or Pilates or what ever exercise fits nicely into your life, can you admit that it's ok to fail? Of course, I don't want you to fail, (and I want your marriage to work out for you too!) but when you are making a commitment to someone, yourself or someone else, you should not be thinking about potential failure in the future. Commit to the gym like you are in love, so in love with your future body and health that nothing can stand in the way.

Please Don't Try

I hear it all the time when coaching — I'll try. "No you won't," I say, "you will acknowledge Yoda from Star Wars wise words: 'Do or do not, there is no try.'"

Make a commitment or go home. 'Try' is not even half a commitment, it's leaving the back door open and it's a waste of your time and mine. Delete the word 'try' from your vocabulary. It's a weak word that has no place in your new life. When you utter the word 'try' you are leaning towards failure. Your options are the following: I am going to give it everything I've got or I am going to wait until I'm ready to commit. Are you ready to make your vows?

To make the right decision there are, however, a few things you need to consider.

Is It A Priority?

When you set out on a journey for change, there are usually many things you want to do. Maybe it's writing, singing or reading but if you start to do too many things at the same time, the odds won't be in your favour. Incremental change is much more powerful and long lasting than massive change all at once. Therefore, the biggest decision you have to make is this; what goal do I want to give my full focus to first?

What are your options? Which habit do you think will have the biggest impact on your life right now? I used to struggle between whether I would focus on the habit of meditation or exercise first. Many times I tried to do the two at once, many times I failed until I finally made a choice. I decided that meditation was going to have the biggest impact on my life right now, it wasn't that I was planning to do no exercise but my morning routine was to include meditation without fail. Meditation was my priority for the coming months. After a couple of months when I felt like I had mastering the habit, then exercise became my focus.

Information Versus Gut Instinct

Some decisions are best made without spending too much time gathering information, others need time and thought to help you decide. There are times when you will know instinctively what should come next, like I did, but for a long time I fought the internal voice that said, master the habit of meditation.

What happened when I finally listened to my intuition? Once I started to mediate regularly, I became calmer, which in turn meant I was more focused, clearer in my vision. When I sat to write, the writing came easier. I slowed down and my achievements started to speed up. When I created the habit of meditation, I came out of my sessions refreshed and feeling good which enabled me to stack the habit of exercise on top of my existing habit.

When I listened to my gut, I made the right decision. So if you want to follow your instinct, just go quiet and listen. Choose one of the habits you want to create and listen to how that makes you feel. Try another one and listen again. Listen with your heart and your soul and you will hear the answer.

What's The Other Option?

If you are finding it difficult to hear your inner voice or you're always confused when it comes to making the right decision, you may want to take some time to consider the consequences of each decision. Write down all of the goals you want to achieve. Consider the reason why you want them? Then look at the habits that are necessary to create to achieve these goals. With each goal ask yourself; what will happen if I create this habit? How will I feel, how will my life change? What will happen if I don't do it? Continue to consider the consequences of every course of action? The more clarity you have the more questions answered the more likely you will make the right decision.

Knowing What's Best

Most of us have well-meaning family members and friends who think they know what is best for us... and there are times in life when they may be right. They may know exercise is going to help you to regain your energy and vitality for life. They may know that meditation will help you to be calmer and more focused but what they don't know is what will work for you and your circumstances right now. Only you can know that. So don't depend on someone else to make your decisions, when you do this you are handing away your power. By all means talk things through with a friend or family member but don't take their opinion on board if it doesn't feel right.

No Choice

Sometimes an external trigger in life gives us no option but to change. This can be a health scare or an emotional breakdown that brings us to a place where change is our only viable option. This can do one of two things; it can be a powerful motivator. Helping give us a solid 'why' for our new habits or it can come with a reluctance, almost a resentment that your choice has been taken away from you. Any negative emotions associated with your new habit should be dealt with if you want to have long-term success. Resistance will not only make the habit routine unpleasant but will inevitably lead to you quitting as soon as you get the opportunity.

Making A Commitment

When you have made the decision on what to focus, it's time to commit. It doesn't have to be a massive commitment to exercise every day till the end of time but a manageable one – one that can fit into your schedule. Maybe it's a 10-minute walk or five press ups a day. Whatever decision you make to start off with, it has to be one that you know you can do whatever the weather. And the only way to prove to yourself that you have made the commitment is to take action. Small every day action is much more powerful that an elaborate plan to change. Taking small steps daily will create the momentum you need to see the benefits of change.

What is your decision? What habit is your number one priority? Which one is going to have the biggest impact on your life.

_____

_____

Fill in the **Decision** section of your **Habit Canvas** on Page 160, what habit are you going to commit to?

Fixed days and times will avoid the 'I'll do it tomorrow' lie we all tell ourselves

7

Designing The Change

Habit Design

WITH a strong desire and the decision made, you must now focus on designing your habit. Habit design will ensure your success. When, where, how and who are some of the questions you will need answered to design your habit. As you answer the questions in each part of this section on habit design remember to fill in your **Habit Canvas** on Page 160.

When

Decide exactly what you are going to do and when you are going to do it. Fixed days and times will avoid the "I'll do it tomorrow" lie we all tell ourselves. If you are forming a new habit it is sometimes better to do a little every day rather than a lot twice or three times a week. Regular practice will help form the habit more quickly. In the example of exercise once you get started and begin to experience the many benefits of regular exercise you will crave the extra energy and feel good factor daily. Let's say you decide you are going to workout every day for 15 minutes. Are you going to do it everyday or every second day? What time of the day will you do it?

Where

Are you going to exercise at home or at the gym? If you decide to do it at home, what room will you exercise in? Make sure the location is realistic and won't ever be a barrier to you carrying out the habit. Making these decisions in advance is fundamental to your success. The clearer you are about the when and where, the better. If you leave it to chance, chances are you will leave it.

Who Will Hold You Accountable?

To reinforce your commitment to your new habit, make it public, nothing motivates humans more than the desire to prove themselves to others. Statistics are poor for people who try to change habits on their own. Your chances increase when you tell someone you know. They increase substantially when you commit to an acquaintance, maybe a coach, a work associate or a mentor. This is a step that many leave out, meaning they can quit whenever they want to. They have no one to face up to only themselves. The reason why some people avoid the accountability partner is because they haven't actually made the decision. They are still in the 'try' zone. They don't want to tell anyone in case they fail. Your decision must be strong, your commitment real. When this is the case, you won't mind sharing your goals with others because you know you will do everything in your power to make it so.

What Are You Willing To Give Up?

Let's be honest for a minute, why hasn't it worked before? Surely you can tell what your typical pitfalls are. This is important because you don't want to keep making the same mistakes. What can you do to make it work this time? If there are people who stand in your way, avoid them, if late movies prevent you from getting up to exercise, stop watching them.

Sometimes it's not what you fail to do but what you fail to NOT do that damages your chances of success. If you are not willing to stop eating chips, chances are you will not loose any weight. If you are not willing to go to bed before 12, chances are you will never become a true member of the 5 a.m. club. Think about what existing habits you have that could ruin your chances of being successful with your future goal. Decide what you are willing to give up in order to achieve your goal. Then take responsibility for the attainment of your goals and stop blaming failure on your lack of commitment.

The Habit Loop

When designing your habit, it's important to take into account a simple loop that Researchers at MIT discovered to be at the core of human behaviour. Habits all consist of a cue and the positive reinforcement of a reward, Charles Duhigg popularised this Habit loop in his book The Power of Habit.

In Duhigg's book, he describes 'The Habit Loop' where each habit consists of a cue, a routine and a reward. The habit of brushing your teeth consists of the cue, tooth film, the routine, brushing your teeth and the reward, a tingling fresh sensation in your mouth.

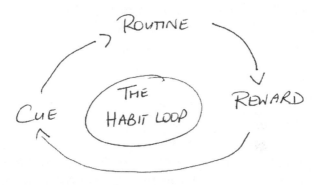

Duhigg claims that by understanding and tapping into the habit loop we can create habits more effortlessly but it can also help us to break unhealthy habits. Take for example the habit of checking emails hundreds of times a day. The cue of the email alert initiated a routine of checking email and the reward? Maybe it was some pleasant news once received in an email or the simple distraction from work that keeps us going there. Removing the alert interrupts the habit loop.

Triggers (The Cue)

A trigger is something that you do every day that you can associate with a new habit to encourage you to complete it. By linking your habit to a trigger, it will help you to remember to carry out your daily routine.

If you want to start meditating, get up in the morning, use the bathroom and then start your meditation. Going to the bathroom is your trigger. Something that you do every morning, once it is done your brain knows it is time to start meditating.

If you want to drink more water, every time you stand up from your desk go fill up your glass. Standing up can trigger the habit of filling up your glass.

If you want to start running in the morning, prepare your running gear the night before and put it beside the bed. Your trigger for the morning is your gear ready to go.

Triggers can be time based, physical objects put in your path, an alarm, a post it note or an existing habit. Existing habits can sometimes be the most powerful triggers (see habit stacking below). Once you have decided on your routine and your trigger, you need to think about the reward.

Rewards

Some habits give natural rewards in the form increased endorphins from exercise, or the natural weight loss that will occur when you eat healthy food. But for the habit reward to work, it must be instant and sufficient to stimulate you into repeating the action again and again. Rewards can be physical, emotional or can come as little treats such as a cup of coffee or a nice breakfast after your workout.

Whatever it is, the brain must crave the reward. If you get to the stage where craving occurs, you have clinched it. It's the craving that drives our behaviour.

Runners crave the endorphin-rush they get from running. I've seen friends get anxious before their nightly run. They are incapable of relaxing until they get their craved reward, endorphins. We have learnt to crave the fresh feeling of mint on our breath after brushing our teeth. We crave the distraction of an email or tweet and we pine for the relaxation from the glass of wine on a Friday evening. All of these habits occur because of the reward yearned.

Keystone Habits

Duhigg also speaks about a certain type of habit which he calls a 'Keystone Habit." These are habits that can encourage other habits. Take the habit of rising early, if you can master getting up early you, will find it easier to create a new habit in this time now available to you. Exercise is also a keystone habit, a lot of people say when they exercise they are more likely to make better food choices, they sleep better and have more energy creating an environment for success. Exercise is one of the strongest keystone habits as it has a tendency to set off a chain reaction which benefits every area of your life.

Think of the opposite, when you don't exercise, you suffer more stress, you are too tired to cook so you make unhealthy food choices which leave you with low energy so you don't exercise. I'm sure most people have experienced this type of cycle in their lives at some stage and the only way to break out of it is to start exercising.

With exercise you will gradually create the energy to help you do lots of other good stuff. Other keystone habits include making your bed in the morning, planning your schedule, meditation and positive thinking can all trigger other positive habits without too much work.

Habit Stacking

Once you have mastered one habit it's time for some habit stacking. Habit stacking is the act of using the momentum of one habit to support the creation of a subsequent habit. If you have managed to create the habit of early rising it is going to be much easier to start to exercise in that time. Use one established habit to trigger the next so if you have mastered meditation why not add five minutes of journaling to your day directly after meditating. It is a great way to make progress without having to go through the trial and error of starting a new habit. You know the time works for you and extending it by five or 10 minutes shouldn't be too difficult.

Tracking; Commit To At Least 21 Days

Tracking your habit will encourage you to stick with it. It acts as both a reminder and a reward. For some myself included the simple act of ticking a box gives great joy. The satisfaction of achievement and the pride when I see a string of ticked boxes. Tracking doesn't have to continue indefinitely, once your habit becomes automatic you can stop tracking. But how long will this take?

There are many figures thrown about as to how long it takes to form a habit. You will hear some say 21 days, others 60 days. The research I'm afraid is not consistent with what we hear. The actual time it takes depends on the individual, the habit to be formed and probably many different factors of which we are still unaware.

Research done by University College London on how habits are formed: *Modelling Habit Formation in The Real World*, looked at the automaticity of habits and how long did it take to form a new habit. Ninety-six volunteers took part in the study and they were given the choice between eating, drinking or an activity behaviour to be carried out daily at the same time for twelve weeks. They recorded their progress and success in a journal and the results differed for many. There was a wide variety of results in the time that it took to make the behaviour automatic. The average time was 66 days with a range from 18 to 254 days.

So if it is not possible to say exactly how long it will take to form a new habit and make it part of your life, why are we constantly told to commit to 21 days?

Sometime in the 1950s a plastic surgeon by the name of Maxwell Maltz noticed that it took his patients about 21 days to get used to their new faces. Amputees also appeared to take a similar time to stop suffering from phantom limb. He wrote about this is his book Psycho Cybernetics and surmised that it requires a minimum of about 21 days for an old mental image to dissolve and a new one to jell.' He went on to say "Our self-image and our habits tend to go together. Change one and you will automatically change the other." Maltz words were misinterpreted to suggested that any habit will take 21 days to form when this was not his intention. But there is truth in the belief that repetitive action is what enables a new habit to form.

If you can commit to taking it on fully for 21 days, it doesn't seem like such a mammoth task. Twenty-one days is short enough to appear doable and long enough to create some sort of momentum. The trick is not to overwhelm yourself starting out. If you have the tendency to avoid hard work or committing to anything that takes longer than five minutes, you have to coax yourself gently into forming a new habit. You can even start with a seven-day challenge and track it so that you can celebrate your success at the end of the week. You might be surprised at how different you feel when you get to the end of the week.

Celebrate
Part of the 'habit loop' is the reward. A way to encourage yourself for your achievements and celebrate your success. If you complete a week of workouts, make sure you acknowledge the greatness of what you have done. Do something nice for yourself, you could get a massage, avoid doing anything that will sabotage your long-term success like rewarding yourself with food or alcohol. Working out will give you a natural reward of feeling good and looking great so you may not need to add in the external reward.

Small Things With Big Impact
Start Small
If you have struggled with habits before, the best way forward is to make your habit so small that nothing will discourage you

from doing it. If you want to write, write 100 words each day, if you want to workout do two push ups a day. If you want to run, run for five minutes a day until these habits become too easy that you can increase the quantity or frequency. By starting small, you trick your body into thinking this is easy. About eight years ago, I complained to a friend that I wanted to write a book but I didn't have the time. With three children, two of whom were under two, I was feeling sorry for myself and frustrated by my circumstances. She gave me a simple piece of advice that has stood the test of time.

"Ten minutes a day will write a book," she said.

It took away the fear, the inertia and the procrastination. It removed my excuse of time and left me with no justification for my lack of action. I had to give it a go and write.

My 10 minutes a day created the momentum that led to my first book 'Chaos to Control.'

The 10-minute rule can be used when trying to create any habit and if you want you can change it to a two-minute rule. However big or small you start, make the time so insignificant that you can't opt out.

Think Big, Act Small and you make progress every day.

Remember we get what we focus on, so focus on success and positivity. There is no place for negativity, excuses and guilt.

"Ninety-nine percent of the failures come from people who have the habit of making excuses," George Washington Carver (American botanist and Inventor)

Continue to fill in the **Habit Canvas** (on Page 160).

8

Discipline For Change

I T took me many years to realise that discipline was not a dirty word, to break the connection to pain and suffering and the idea that it involved doing something I don't actually want to do. It was the English that gave discipline it's bad reputation, first used in the 13th century to refer to mortification by scourging oneself... in other words self-flagellation. Fortunately, the Latin roots of the word were much more appealing as they referred to learning and knowledge.

But when we refer to the discipline to pursue the goals we want, we need to look at it through the lens of motivation. To have discipline is simply to maintain continued motivation. When you start a new habit you are motivated, you are clear about why you want to create the habit and you feel good about pursuing it. Self-discipline or willpower is not required because motivation is strong. If you could remind yourselves of your motivation regularly, you may never need self-discipline.

But because we are human beings there will be the days where we don't want to think about what motivates us or to be logical about what's good for us. These are the days that true habit will benefit us. Thanks to the Neuroplasticity of the brain we have the ability to change and grow at any age or stage of our lives. The old excuses of 'I am who I am' or 'you can't teach an old dog new tricks' will no longer give you the excuse you need not to get up off your ass.

So if we are carried by our pre-programmed habits, why do we need discipline at all? Because realistically there will be times where we question the logic of our logical habits. There will be times that we don't feel great or we have a better options open to us. These are the days when discipline is required. The discipline to quieten the negative thoughts and persist with the plan.

Discipline Starts With Making The Right Decision

It's easier to employ self-discipline when you know you are on the right path. If you choose to run a marathon, it is very clear what you need to do to achieve that goal. If you choose to start a business, get healthy or be a nicer person, these goals are a little more open to interpretation and unless you get specific about what exactly that means to you, you are less likely to be successful with your goal.

A nutrition coach I know switched from working with adolescent athletes to working in the corporate environment. He had great success with the young athletes, when he gave his advice and explained how certain changes in their diet would amount to weight gain or more muscle mass, the results would be visible in weeks. When he switched to the corporate environment, the same good advice, often to lose weight or create muscle didn't seem to create the same results. What he realised was that the young athletes had a very clear purpose. They had clear goals and understood that certain actions would give them the results that they wanted. The corporate workers didn't have such compelling goals. Weight loss or a better body doesn't appear to be as tangible or as desirable for an office worker who also likes to eat out and party often. Your goal needs to be a priority in order to ensure you take action towards its accomplishment.

Discipline Means Not Questioning The Process

I often see people who set a goal and put a lot of work into planning out the steps that are going to get them there. Then every day after that, they spend precious time questioning the plan, convincing themselves that three days in the gym is sufficient, four is probably not necessary or that six o'clock is unnecessarily early, 6:30 is probably fine. There may be the odd occasion where the plan you have laid out for yourself needs tweaking or an event in your life might steer you in a different direction. Nine times out of ten if you have decided on good information to reach your goal, don't argue with yourself... just do it.

Discipline Helps You Overcome The Bad Days

There will be days when you are too tired, too lazy or full of self-pity to follow through but these are the days that you need to be strong. You need to find that strength inside to overcome the negative self-talk when your brain is screaming at you to take a break, to skip today, and get back to it tomorrow. Take note: these are the traps, these are the obstacles your brain will throw your way to avoid the discomfort and resist the change. Recognise this and fight back.

Just for today continue with your habit, do your training, your writing, your healthy eating and if you still need a break tomorrow, take it tomorrow. Win today's battle and feel that sense of pride and accomplishment that you had the mental strength to say 'no,' Just as you don't think twice about taking a shower or brushing your teeth, make your new habit a compulsory part of your day. I've got to the stage where I know that meditation and exercise are part of my life, they are as essential to my well-being as eating healthy and sleeping, so when I hear my bull rearing its head in my weak moment, I turn to her and say — "Not a option."

Discipline Overpowers Immediate Gratification

Another great challenge is to put off immediate gratification to see the long-term success. Tim Urban of waitbutwhy.com says that we all have an instant gratification monkey that hijacks our rational decision-making brain and makes us do enjoyable things that actually turn out to be not so enjoyable because they are shrouded in guilt! When we stay focused on the end goal, we are more likely to be able to banish the instant gratification monkey and do what we need to do stay focused on the long-term goal...keep your goals close by to remind yourself of you what and your why?

Discipline Helps You Rise Before Your Bull

The best strategy for maintaining discipline is to 'Rise before your Bull.' Every time you hesitate when you know you should be doing something, stand up and disrupt the negative thoughts that you know are coming. Don't listen to the excuses or loopholes that are coming next. By shifting your thoughts away from the excuses which were about to bombard you, you can acknowledge that the bull was about to start and focus positively on the habit that you know you should be carrying out. Don't give the negative and self-sabotaging thoughts an opportunity to take hold. Take back the control by 'Rising before your Bull!'

Discipline is the bridge between goals and accomplishment, and if you want to be among a group of elite humans who have a rare strength to overcome their own mind and stay focused on their success, you too will embrace discipline.

Habits Reduce The Need For Discipline And Decision Making

President Obama was known to wear the same colour suits and eat the same menu daily. "I don't want to make decisions about what I am eating or what I am wearing as I have too many important decisions to make," he said.

He understood the cognitive load each decision takes and the limited capacity of the human brain, therefore he decided not to waste any of this processing power on futile decision making. We do it all the time in work, we spend our days reacting and using email as a to do list rather than making upfront decisions about priorities and scheduling our work. If we were to do this we would reduce the need to make decisions every half and hour what will I do next? Decision fatigue is a real phenomenon that most busy people suffer from. Ever stand in the supermarket after work and can't make your mind up what to have for dinner? By evening time most of us have used up our decision making capacity.

In one particular study, researchers looked at more than 1,100 parole hearing decisions made by judges in the U.S. What they found was that the time their case was heard was more influential in the outcome than the crime itself or the person's background. The earlier in the day the case was heard, the more likely parole would be granted. The mental work of ruling on case after case wears the decision-maker down and the choices you make later in the day become more difficult. The more decisions you need to make during the day, the worse you're going to be at weighing all the options and making an informed choice by the end of the day.

While its best to make your most important decisions earlier in the day, if you create habits such as planning your recurring tasks, you free up your brain for the more important decisions and problem solving.

Discipline For High Performance

High performance is achieving or accomplishing more than the average over the long-term. High performers do what most don't or won't do... they outperform the masses.

Most high performers have a number of habits that define them. They may have habits relevant to their job or their hobbies. Habits that fuel their days with positive results.

Football legend Cristiano Ronaldo continuously outperforms his peers. Most professional footballers would have similar training routines but Ronaldo reckons his warm-down routine is what sets him apart from the rest.

"Recovery is more important to me than actual training sessions due to the large number of games I have to play. Winding down and resting is a key part of my day-to-day routine and enables me to perform to the highest level in my profession and prolong my career."

In an interview with Spanish sports newspaper *AS*, Ronaldo outlined his post-match routine which included the following, all available at home in his mansion in Madrid.

As soon as the match is over, he starts to refuel with fruit and foods rich in carbohydrates and protein. He then engages in 'contrast therapy' which is bathing in cycles of cold and hot water. The idea is to stimulate blood flow in areas that may have suffered injury or strain. It also acts as an anti-inflammatory reducing any bruising from his game. He allegedly then jumps in his pool for a 20-minute swim followed by high pressured water therapy and a Turkish bath.

Ronaldo is just one of many successful people who have regular habits that dictate their lives. Deepak Chopra wakes at 4am and meditates for two hours. Will Smith says his exercise routine means he is always ready. Tony Robbins includes 'Gratitude' in morning routine.

Successful people practice daily habits. The interesting thing is that most of their routines are not outside our reach. It's not necessary to meditate for as long as Deepak to get the benefits of meditation. Neither do we need to work out like Ronaldo to profit from exercise. What sets the high performers apart from the rest is their discipline. It takes discipline to stick with a habit before you see the results. High performers commit to repeatedly doing the actions that they know serve them. Getting up to exercise when they went to bed too late or meditating when they feel like watching TV. The secret to high performance for most of us doesn't have to involve increasing your hours of practice but ensuring the consistency of daily practice. Because when most are making excuses because they don't feel like it, you have shown up to do what you need to do.

What are the excuses or loopholes you use to avoid doing what you said you would do?

_____

_____

What will you do when you don't feel like it?

_____

_____

Transfer your answers to the **Habit Canvas** on Page 160.

9

Giraffes And Their Necks

JEAN-BAPTISTE LAMARCK was a French biologist who some believe had a better claim to the theory of evolution than Charles Darwin. Lamarck proposed that organisms acquire and pass on adaptations necessary for their survival in a changing environment. Take the giraffe for example, As it wanders the plains of Africa scouring for food, a lot of the best food at lower heights had been eaten by other, possibly more dominant animals. The only food available is in the higher branches so the giraffe stretches itself and its neck to try to reach the higher branches. Lamarck believed that over generations this habit of reaching and stretching would produce giraffes with longer necks and legs to enable it to feed comfortably.

Sounds plausible?

Back in Lamarck's time not too many thought so, he was first denounced as a heretic by the church and then ridiculed by his fellow scientists, the majority of whom were of course creationists. A German biologist by the name of Weismann made sure his theory was totally discredited when over five years he tested what he believed to be Lamarck's theory by cutting off the tails of mice in the hope that the next generation would be born with no tail. He did this with 22 generations of mice and they continued to have tails. Nobody considered the fact that mice might actually need their tails.

Darwin's theory of natural selection believed that all organisms are different from each other and these variations lead to the likelihood of survival or not. If an animal has features that make it more likely to survive or reproduce, it is more likely to pass on these traits to the next generation. With the evolutions of genetics and the discovery of the human genome, Darwin's theory was strengthened. For many years, we got caught up in the possibility that our fate was predetermined in our genes. But we now understand the difference between correlation and causation and that our genes don't necessarily cause our illnesses alone. There are, of course, cases such as cystic fibrosis or Huntington's disease which can be blamed entirely on the gene. With the birth of epigenetics, research has established that DNA blueprints passed down through genes are not set in stone at birth and that we might inherit learned traits. Lamarck may have been a little bit right, so the experts say and environmental influences do have an effect.

It also appears that Darwin had realised the significant impact of the environment in 1876 when he admitted in a letter he wrote to Moritz Wagner that he hadn't put enough emphasis on the environment, food, climate etc. independently to natural selection.

Your Environment

So all roads appear to point to the fact that the environment plays a massive role in making us who we are and our ancestors, children and pets who they are. The food we eat, the air we breathe, the job we do all constitute our environment.

Are you stressed at work and eating poorly or practicing yoga daily and eating a healthy wholefood diet?

The second environment is going to be much more conducive to creating any new habits that will ensure you remain healthy and fit. Before you make any decisions about what habits you are going to implement, you need to take your environment into account.

If you have a nine to five job and you need to leave your house at 7:30 every morning, these realities make it easy to accept the habit of rising at 6:30. You don't have much choice in the matter. If you are a freelance web designer working from home, it is going to be a little more difficult to establish the habit of rising of 6:30.

The type of job you have will also have differing levels of acceptable behaviours and certain routines that need to be carried out without fail. If you are a prison guard, your daily work habits will be pretty strict and there won't be much space for improvisation or tweaking of your timetable. Nurses, social workers, bus drivers all live with rigid processes that must be carried out whatever the weather.

There are a host of habits that soldiers adopt when part of the military from making their beds in the morning to taking their hats off indoors. Some of the habits soldiers learn become engrained, they have been hardwired into their subconscious mind, automated and difficult to change. Others would be more difficult to maintain outside the military as the environment plays a large part in establishing and maintaining those habits.

Think of your life at the moment, do you work long hours? Do you have small children that keep you awake at night? There are many factors in the life that you are living that you will need to take into consideration before you make your decision. If you have the burning desire and you know against the odds that you want to form this habit, then you must design the habit to fit into your environment. When I first tried to create the habit of meditation, my children were small and woke very early. I tried many times to wake earlier than them but I could never get any momentum going and it only made me more frustrated and disappointed with myself. I had tried to get up earlier than the kids and that hadn't worked so I started to do it late at night when they had gone to bed. You have to design your new habits to fit your environment.

Designing Your Environment For Success

There are ways in which you can design your environment to support the implementation of your new habits. Here are a number of suggestions.

Design For Productivity

Think about the design of your office. Design it in a way that encourages you to get work done. Office design is a bit like kitchen design, make sure the things you use most frequently are within your reach. Put your most unused items in the farthest away cupboard. Your filing cabinet should be accessible, otherwise you can be sure you will have a massive pile of filing at the end of the year. Make it easier to do the jobs you hate. Put some thought into your comfort.

Desks

Make sure your office desk is fit for purpose. If you use a laptop only you won't have a need for a large desk but if your work involves paper work or creativity, you may need a larger desk to make it easier to work. Sometimes we avoid making changes because we think the cost outweighs the benefits but if the right equipment would make your life easier and make you more creative and productive, upgrade your desk. Standing desks are all the mode currently. The belief is that standing desks increase productivity but the research is inconclusive at best. Some people swear by them especially those with back issues, so you may want to try it out or you could make one yourself by putting a small coffee table onto of your desk just to try it out.

Comfortable Seating

A comfortable office chair is so important and even more so if you sit at your desk all day long. Make sure you have the support you need. You could try out a fitness ball, you can even buy nice coloured covers for them so you don't have a luminous orange chair under your butt attracting too much attention.

Lighting

Natural light, of course, is ideal but if you don't have a natural light source, consider buying a good lamp and make sure that the light is bright enough to enable you to do your best work.

Technology

Having the technology to help you to work efficiently is something we often forget to consider. Is your computer causing frustration? Do you have the right software to do your job. All impact your productivity and efficiency.

Phones

Do you have your email and social media notifications switched off? When you are trying to do some important work can you switch off your phone? Simple actions can eliminate distractions and ensure a better environment for focus.

Headphones

One of the most useful presents I have every received are my blue tooth ear buds. When I need to focus, I plug them in and listen to chill sounds or peaceful piano. It helps me create the environment for focus.

Design For Sleep

If you want to improve your sleep habits you may need to take control of your bedroom environment. If you have a TV in the bedroom I suggest removing it, that does not mean you have permission to watch movies on your laptop, tablet or phone! A good sleep routine is essential for a good night's sleep and also for creating a morning routine. So if you want to create the habit of rising early, you will need to take some time to look at your bedtime habits. Just treat yourself like you would a baby, don't eat too late at night, don't do anything that might excite you or stimulate you before sleep.

Design For Healthy Eating

Take a look inside your kitchen cupboards. Are the contents supporting your attempts at healthy eating or do you have one too many temptations lying around? Don't buy food you don't want to eat and if you are only buying it for your kids should they be eating it at all? Leave healthy snacks accessible and put them in containers that make them look more attractive. Consider baking healthy snacks in advance for all the family. Make your kitchen a healthy zone.

Design For Reading More

If you want to read more, strategically place the books you have wanted to read for a while around the house. Put your TV remote in the cupboard and leave a book on a coffee table close to where you sit in your living room. If you don't have a coffee table leave it on your chair. You could also leave a book on your pillow in the morning to remind you to read it when you go to bed. Little triggers can be placed in your environment to encourage you to do the habits that you want to do. Remove the temptations from view and make your new positive habits more attractive with reminders and encouragement.

What needs to change in your environment to support your new habit?

_____

_____

Transfer your answers to the **Habit Canvas** on Page 160.

10

The Ritual Cat

WHEN the spiritual teacher and his disciples began their evening meditation, the cat who lived in the monastery made so much noise that it distracted them. So the teacher ordered that the cat be tied up during the evening practice. Years later, when the teacher died, the cat continued to be tied up during the meditation session. And when the cat eventually died, another cat was brought to the monastery and tied up. Centuries later, descendants of the spiritual teacher wrote scholarly treatises about the religious significance of tying up a cat for meditation practice.

How many futile rituals are in your life which have been handed down through the generations? As a large portion of our lives are lived on autopilot, we have many pointless and ineffective habits that we replay over and over and often lead us to not get the results we want from life.

Breaking Bad Habits

It's only in recent years that when we say the word habit it's more likely to be interpreted in a positive context. For many years when we spoke about habit it was regularly a reference to a negative unhealthily behaviour. Smoking, drinking, gambling, overeating, drug abuse, all repetitive behaviours that have a negative impact on the individual's life. Fortunately, we are now more aware of what habits are and how we can break the chain of negative habits and strengthen the links of the positive sort. A lot of exploration has been done into the subject of addiction and how to break these destructive patterns. Creating new positive habits appears to be a significant part of solution.

We know that habits take many forms — there are the habitual behaviours that we have grown accustomed to that give us temporary gratification. There are also the habitual thoughts about who we are and what that means in the world and there are habitual emotions. Emotions we have become addicted to because of the chemical connections in our body that crave these familiar emotions even if they aren't good for us.

Most of us have habits that are negatively impacting our happiness and success. It could be a little bad habit of checking Facebook first thing is the morning or something more significant like smoking or excessive drinking. Breaking bad habits starts with understanding the different components of the habit formation.

Understanding The Triggers

Each habit has a habit loop, trigger, behaviour and reward. Become aware of the trigger, when do you reach for the biscuit jar, is it boredom? Is it a time trigger? perhaps it's hunger and a lack of planning alternative snacks. There are many reasons why we behave the way we do. Get to the root of why you do what you do and you can better control the habitual patterns.

Changing The Environment

Some environments trigger certain actions so if you are triggered by a certain place or being with certain people, change the environment. Don't bring the kids to a McDonalds restaurant for lunch if you have started a healthy eating regime. We associate certain behaviors with certain locations and this will trigger us to behave in a certain way. A new house, a new place of work, a new town all give plenty of scope for changing old routines and habits. If you are trying to change an old habit, consider what you can do to change the environment in which the bad habit occurs. If you don't want to eat chocolate, don't buy it. If you don't want to eat desert don't look at the dessert menu. Create an environment that is going to support you and not hinder your success. Surround yourself with the people who will support you in breaking bad habits and encouraging the good.

Avoid Drastic Action

Remember just like you need to create new habits with tiny steps, breaking bad habits can be done incrementally also. Sometimes if we have bad habits, we think we need to eliminate them completely but maybe our bad habits wouldn't be so bad if we could decrease their frequency of use. For example, a glass of wine doesn't have to be a bad habit if it is done moderately and for positive reasons. So rather than giving up wine totally, can you reduce the amount you consume and the frequency and still enjoy the wine? Some people have stopped smoking by gradually reducing the amount they smoked each day. Other habits such as too much social media or not cleaning up after dinner can also be approached gradually.

For example, if you need to break the habit of Facebook, you could limit yourself to certain times of the day. Replace nighttime social media by buying a new book and leave it beside your bed to read each night.

If you are in the habit of leaving the dishes after your evening meal, why not commit to cleaning them just one night a week, then two and what you will find is the reward of clean kitchen will eventually outweigh your tiredness at night.

Replacing The Bad With The Good

One of the most popular methods of breaking a bad habit is to replace it with a better one. It is very difficult to just stop doing something so people have more success when they give themselves something else to focus on.

Bad Eating Habits

Food habits are easy to find a replacement for. You can shift from biscuits to nuts, or a Greek yoghurt. Substitute hummus and veg sticks for crisps. There are plenty of healthy tasty treats that you can replace your bad eating habits with and tons of good websites that will help you to do that.

Overindulging In Alcohol

If pouring a glass a wine is the first thing you do when you get home from work, think about what else you could do instead of the wine. Could you replace it with a cup of coffee or maybe with a soda water and lime?

Staying Up Too Late

Is late night TV your curse? Can you create a habit of taking a relaxing bath or going to bed with a new book that you want to read.

Smoking

Many people have successfully given up smoking by taking up running or a sport that increases endorphins and dopamine. It may have a hard time beating the nicotine fix but it definitely will help.

Breaking The Habit Of Negative Thoughts?

Most people think of bad habits as physical ones like the examples above but in my experience the habitual unhelpful thoughts can be more damaging. It's easier to change what you can see and often we are unaware that our thoughts can also be habits.

When you wake up in the morning what's on your mind? Hey, it's a new day, an opportunity to start fresh and have fun. Or do you wake groaning, wishing you could stay in bed? What about mid-morning, lunchtime and later in the day? Take note of what you are thinking and decide if it's what you would like to fill your world with.

Change Your Thoughts, Change Your World

Can changing your thoughts really change your world? Quantum physics, epigenetics and the placebo effect point in this direction. Our thoughts have an energy attached to them and some say, give us the ability to heal ourselves, feel better and ultimately change the reality around us. Henry Ford implied it many years ago: "If you think you can or you think you can't, you are probably right." You can make or break your world just by your thinking. Some of you will already be using these theories to change your world. For some of you, these concepts probably sound crazy but I would encourage you to investigate the subject some more and open your mind to the possibilities. You might be surprised at how aligning your thoughts and your actions can give you exponential results.

One of the books that has had a powerful impact on helping me break the negative patterns is *Breaking the Habit of Being Yourself* by Dr. Joe Dispenza. He outlines how your genes do not determine future outcomes and shows how we can work towards creating a new reality using meditation.

Mindfulness As A Strategy

Judson Brewer, associate professor in psychiatry at the school of medicine at Brown University, developed mindfulness programmes for habit change including treatments for smoking, emotional eating and anxiety. Our Pre frontal cortex understands on an intellectual level that we shouldn't smoke or eat 10 cookies in a row but our prefrontal cortex is the first to go off line when we are stressed. When this happens, we are more likely to fall back on our more primitive parts of the brain, making us quicker to anger, overreact and become more emotional. As this more primitive part of the brain is responsible for our habits, this is why we fall back into habitual patterns so easily. Our emotional triggers to eat have been created in our brains without our awareness. Feel sad, eat chocolate, feel better. It's not just hunger that triggers us to eat but sadness, boredom, overwhelm. Many emotions can trigger our desire for food which gives us comfort.

Brewer speaks about his Mindful Smoking programme on his 2015 Ted Talk. He said while people intellectually know smoking is bad for them, only when they mindfully smoke does it help make the connection in the brain of how disgusting the habit actually is. Mindfulness helps you to see clearly the results of your actions. Mindfulness is about understanding what is happening in your body and mind from moment to moment, being aware of all your thoughts, emotions and actions.

His strategy is to get curious. To step away from the fear-based reactive habit patterns and to understand what is triggering your actions. Notice all urges and get curious about why they are occurring. He says that cravings are simply body sensations — we should recognise them and try to understand them.

What Are The Habits That Prevent Your Success?

So what habit would you like to break? You can use the **Habit Canvas** (Page 160) to help you to break a bad habit by understanding what's triggering it. It could be the environment you are in, it could be unhappiness or grief or it could simply be boredom. When you are clear about the component parts, you can work to break the damaging patterns. In my experience the best way to break a bad habit is to focus on a good one to replace it. By focusing on something new and positive, you increase your chances of the bad habit reducing its power and attractiveness.

PART 3

Modelling The Habits Of The Greats

Increase your chance of success and happiness

So what are the habits that will increase your chances of success and happiness? While the answer to this question is a personal matter there are some habits that most successful people and top performers practice daily.

I have separated these habits into three different types of habits — Productivity Habits, Energy Habits and Presence Habits.

Productivity Habits include planning and scheduling, focus, Email management, staying clutter free.

Energy Habits make for a better life include exercise and nutrition and sleep.

Presence Habits that will improve your well-being include; the practice of Gratitude, Meditation, and Mindfulness.

There will, of course, be other habits that will be relevant to you at different times of your life and in different job roles, you will have different requirements but these habits are the ones that can give you energy, improve well-being and if persisted with, will improve your happiness levels throughout your life.

11

Productivity Habits

The Habit Of Planning

Prior to using my calendar, I was stressed out, frustrated and always disappointed in myself. There was so much I wanted to create but couldn't manage to take action. Since making scheduling part of my weekly planning process, I have achieved so much and feel more in control of my life. For me this was my No. 1 keystone habit because it enabled a lot of other great things to unfold. The following are several ways you can benefit from using a calendar.

Beating Procrastination

Like most people, you probably have a list of things you'd like to do but never find the time to do. Maybe you'd like to write a book, do yoga or start playing guitar. The chief reason people give for never doing the things that they want to do with their lives is that they don't have time. They fill their days with daily tasks and convince themselves that they're too tired to spend their free time pursuing their goals and dreams.

The truth is you have more time available than you realise. Using the calendar has helped me to identify this time. It has helped me to become aware of all the hours in my day and use them more effectively. If there's something you've wanted to do for a long time, schedule some time into your calendar to get started. Once you make a start on something, you're much more likely to keep going.

Assisting Focus

The calendar helps me to focus. When I have planned an activity and know how much time I need, entering it in to my calendar greatly assists my focus. I have commit to completing this activity, so unless something more important crops up, that is what I will be doing at that time. Planning with the calendar helps me to get in touch with the big picture. When you can see what the overall goal is that you're trying to achieve, it is more motivating and inspiring to go get it.

Getting More Organised

The calendar is also a way to get more organised. When your work is planned, you can visualise more clearly what needs to be done. This helps you to distribute your work more evenly throughout the week and keeps you more organised and in control. This can be very empowering in a work environment. When you can see how your time is spent you are more aware of your capacity. When you are clear about your capacity, it's easier to set boundaries.

Creating Alignment With Goals

Planning your week in advance means you're less likely to let time-wasting tasks disturb your day. If you look back at the past week and work out how you spent your time, you'll soon see whether the tasks that you do each day are in alignment with your big goals and supporting their achievement. Make sure that you're making progress toward your goals and that you've scheduled time every day to help you make that progress.

Some of the things that should go into your calendar:

Meetings: These can even include coffee dates with friends or meetings with your family. All meetings should be noted and planned for in your calendar. By relying on your calendar and not on your mind to remember your meetings, you free up thinking time to get more creative in your meetings.

Medical appointments: Dentist, doctor and specialist appointments fall into this category. It's best to leave extra time on either side of these appointments. More often than not, this type of meeting doesn't start on time and therefore has the tendency to run over time.

Holidays: It's important to block off holiday time in your calendar as soon as possible. Blocking off the holiday time encourages you to commit to taking a holiday rather than deciding you are too busy and keep pushing through.

The Weekly Review: If you don't currently do a weekly review, you can look into David Allen's weekly review from the book 'Getting Things Done: The Art of Stress-Free Productivity.' It's important to schedule a period of time once per week to process your inbox and review your goals and priorities so you can feel in control of your workload. Set aside an hour every week to get this done.

Exercise: Using your calendar to plan your workouts will prompt you to stick to your schedule.

Strategic Thinking Time: Not one executive I have met has enough time to do all the tasks required of him. What I notice more and more is that most managers are in reactive mode. They react to the work that comes their way. Very little time is put into planning and even less time given to strategic thinking. If you're in a senior management position, part of your job is to spend time thinking about how your organisation or team can improve and grow.

Plan some strategic thinking time into your calendar each week. Even if you have to leave the office to go to a coffee shop or to a park, factor in the time and commit to it. It's as important to the business as doing accounts and shouldn't be left to chance.

Creative Thinking Time: Just as many people spend too little time strategically thinking, people also don't give enough time to creative thinking. It's difficult to be creative in the typical office environment, a place where distraction and interruptions are part of every working hour. Put some creative thinking time in your calendar. Plan a trip to a museum or to a wide open space, sit back, relax and get creative.

Fun Time: I've realised in recent years that if I don't schedule my downtime, it never happens. I've also realised that relaxation is part of my job. If I don't unwind, detach and relax, I don't perform as well as I should. Planning time for fun is as important as planning time for invoicing.

Tips For Using Your Calendar

✱ If you use outlook, set it up to open in calendar and not with your inbox

✱ Plan all priority work in your calendar

✱ Do a weekly review to make sure you have completed all tasks

✱ Don't schedule work you know you are unlikely to do

✱ Sync your calendar with your phone so you have it with you at all times.

The Habit Of Email Management

Email has become a scourge in recent years, absorbing our time and attention. It is drastically overused in the corporate environment. Couple that with the flood of marketing messages we receive each day and you can see why it's important to take control of it all. The first step is to acknowledge that email is not a to-do list. Your email inbox is a place for capturing your email and the tasks to be done inside your emails, but you should then take the work out of your inbox and organise it for action.

Unless your role demands it, avoid leaving your email open all day, as this leaves you more susceptible to getting distracted by a new email or being tempted to have a quick look. Schedule times for processing your email each day. I suggest working with email early morning, again mid morning, after lunch, and before you go home. Of course, this schedule is just a suggestion and will differ according to your job role. Some job roles allow you to take larger gaps between opening your email; others require more regular interaction. Managing your email in this way helps you to move away from the 'always on' culture and move toward an 'always in control' world.

Turning Off Notifications

When your focus is disturbed, estimates say it takes up to 15 minutes to regain your focus. So each time you see an envelope or hear a beep your attention has been disturbed. Switch off your email notifications and while you are at it your social media ones too. The benefit of switching off notifications is that you're no longer a slave to your email. You decide when you're going to your inbox.

Going For Inbox Zero

Inbox zero is a concept created by Merlin Mann of 43 Folders (*www. 43folders.com*). The idea is to touch each email only once, deciding what to do with it there and then. You should also set aside time each day to process your email instead of dipping in and out of your inbox throughout the day. As you check your email, start to plan and organise the work that lies inside each email.

If you plan the work in each email instead of leaving it in your inbox, you can clear out your inbox easily each day. When you reach inbox zero, it's not that all your work is done, it's that all your work is scheduled or organised into the correct folders. People who master the habit feel more in control and organised.

You could also use the 4D method to clear your inbox. (Do, Delegate, Delete or Defer) Start by scanning your email and answering the emails that can be answered in less than two minutes. Spend 10 minutes or so answering non-critical emails and then process some of the emails left over. The idea is to keep trimming the fat without it taking over your day.

Delegate: You can delegate tasks in an email by forwarding it on to someone else or assigning a task directly in your task management programme.

Delete: This doesn't need much explanation but it does need encouragement. Use the delete button as often as possible and try to reduce the number of emails you need to deal with. Take a look at your inbox. How many of the emails you receive daily are of value? How many are from newsletters you don't read or mailing lists you don't need to be a part of? Instead of just deleting them as they arrive, take a few minutes to eliminate them from your inbox forever and hit unsubscribe.

Defer: If you need to defer a task, you need to either put it in your task management system or schedule the work in your calendar.

Do: And don't forget to actually do some of the tasks. Any task that takes less than two minutes can be done straightaway. Alternatively, any task that requires immediate action needs to be attended to.

If your email is not actionable but important, you may need to keep it for reference. Create a filing system for the emails you need to keep. The key is to have as many folders as you need but as few as possible. You don't need to create a folder for each client or each area of work; you can make do with a couple of folders.

Tips For Creating The Habit Of Effective Email Management

* Start the day in your calendar
* Batch process email
* Touch every email once
* Delete emails you don't need
* File emails that you want to keep for reference
* Action emails that require action in Calendar or Task Manager
* Unsubscribe to unwanted email lists
* Use the 4 Ds to clear your inbox regularly

The Morning Routine

Creating a morning routine is one of the best productivity habits you can adopt. It is what enabled me to fit in the two habits that I knew were going to change my life — exercise and meditation. For many years, I'd lost the essence of who I was. I was tired and frustrated. Creating a morning routine helped me to stop feeling sorry for myself and gave me the opportunity to reinvent myself.

Believe me when I say this — if you can manage against all odds to get up early, just like the chief, you will take back the control of your life. Getting up early is not just important from the perspective of the time that you can gain, it's a lot bigger than that. It means you have won the battle. You have overcome adversity. You have proven to yourself that you can be the ruler of your own life, that you have the power to sway all outcomes. Getting up early makes you the leader, the chief, the hero of your own story.

Reset Required

Remember that reprogramming your brain won't happen in one day, nor in one week. Your habits are rooted deep inside you. There are many things that happened to make you the person you are today. I could lay some blame on the Snoopy poster that hung on my bedroom wall. The words which became my mantra, my excuse and eventually my reality.

"I think I'm allergic to mornings."

It's so easy to create your personality around a statement, aligning yourself to a state that excuses you from responsibility. We do it all the time. These silly mantras can become beliefs over time and when we install these beliefs, we give ourselves permission daily to do things that we know are not good for us or that we know we shouldn't do. We justify our behaviour with adopted beliefs about who we think we are.

Each night when setting my alarm clock, I would remind myself of the benefits. How including yoga, meditation and exercise in my morning routine would make me feel. I would take a few minutes to focus on the positive feelings, how proud, content and resilient I feel when it is all complete. When I have mastered the negative and done what I know to be right. I remind myself of the great things that happen when I am in control.

Taking control of your mind is the first step to creating the life that you want. Believing in your own personal power. What could you achieve if you were in control of your day?

Aristotle said: "It is well to be up before daybreak, for such habits contribute to health, wealth, and wisdom."

Many other famous and successful people through the years have shared his view. Writers, politicians and sports stars have used this tactic to achieve great feats. Not only gaining from the extra time that the early riser earns but also from the individual wins of discipline and habit.

Ernest Hemingway declared: "When I am working on a book or story I write every morning as soon after first light as possible. There is no one to disturb you and it is cool or cold and you come to your work and warm as you write..."

Hemingway was one of many writers who enjoyed the tranquillity of the morning and benefitted from that feeling of accomplishment for the rest of the day, having spent a few hours dedicated to his writing early in the day.

Barack Obama and many other politicians were noted for the early morning habits. Obama ensured he hit the gym every morning before going to the office. He didn't try to fit it in, he made time to do it.

Morning Productivity
Early risers are usually the more organised type. An early morning start allows you to focus on your goals and gives you the time to plan how you are going to achieve them. Getting organised gives you an advantage in the world of business.

Burning The Candle
Of course rising early should only happen when the candle hasn't

been burned at the other end. It is not sustainable to stay up late every night and get up early every morning. It is also very difficult to create the habit of rising early if your children are small and have the tendency to disturb your sleep every night. Sleep is an essential element, too little and we cease to function properly. Our mood is affected, our focus, our emotions and our health can all be negatively impacted when we don't get enough sleep. If you are to become an early riser, then going to bed before midnight also has its advantages.

The Early Student Catches Good Grades

Early risers get better grades, according to a study done by the Department of Psychology in a Texas University. A questionnaire was designed to ask students whether they were a morning person or an evening person. If there were no constraints on life when would they go to bed and wake up and when they were most productive. The results showed that the morning people got a better grade average than the evening people. Students who get up early are more likely to get to class on time, whereas students who stay up late have more temptation to go out partying or drinking.

Think about your own life, if you get up early in the morning do you spend this extra time in a productive way or do you waste time on useless activities? Are you more likely to exercise, write or meditate in the morning or the evening?

Rising early has thought me that if I can overcome my biggest challenge, change a habit that I thought was inherent, somehow tied to my DNA, then I can do anything. It has injected a confidence into my veins that nobody can take a way. It's my secret elixir, my arc reactor.

Tips For Creating A Morning Routine
* Go to bed an hour earlier
* Gradually begin one hour earlier – 7am to 6am to 5am
* Decide why you are doing it in advance

* Decide what you are going to do with the time
* Do not Snooze – get out of bed immediately (rise before your bull)
* Wash your face
* Let the daylight in (if there is any)
* Start with one new habit at a time
* Prepare for your habits the night before, (running gear ready if you plan on going for a run)

What About The Night Owls?

These are the people who do their best work at night. Undisturbed, focused and productive.

I am definitely not a night owl as I fall asleep too easily but I often find myself doing very focused and creative work late into the evening when the rest of the house is asleep. The obvious explanation is the stillness. The noise and distractions of the day are gone and I can focus. It's a wonderful time of the day to work undisturbed, you know you have at least six hours before anyone will stir. Just you, the ticking clock and the dripping tap lulling you into an almost meditative state of focus.

So why not do it all the time and benefit from the gifts the night can bring? The problem is if I stay up late writing, the following day I'm exhausted and my late nights which no longer involve drinking and partying take their toll on my state of mind during the day. It's easy to create a pattern of not functioning during the day and waiting until the early hours to blossom into creativity. I believe this is not a long term strategy for success.

The challenge is how can we create the circumstances for pure focus at a different time in the day? Can the early riser benefit from the same stillness and focus that the moon light brings?

If you can get up as early as your body will allow and use this quiet time to create you will create the space to get things done. Doing it in the morning adds to your sense of achievement and your positivity for the day. If by 10 o'clock you have written a couple of thousand words and done a 30 minute workout the rest of the day can only get better.

The problem some people come up against with being creative in the morning is they allow their brain to kick into "To Do mode". So much to do this morning you can't possible focus on writing or anything else for that matter. It's like checking your email first thing in the morning or going on social media before you have done anything for yourself.

If you allow yourself to start thinking about your daily 'To Do' list or allow the thoughts or imaginary smells of breakfast to waft your way, you may not succeed with morning productivity. You must set the stage, create the environment, remove the distractions and only then will you reap the benefits.

You can still stay up late every once in a while if the creative flow hits you. The reality is it depends on your circumstances in life, your age, your responsibilities and commitments. If you are at a stage of life where your time is your own and you are neither answerable nor responsible for anyone but yourself, being a night owl can work. But if you are someone who can't find the time to fit in all that you want to do and are frustrated by life and not achieving your goals, then consider this.

Rise before your bull and see how your life will change for the better. Your early mornings will be led by you. You get to decide what you do with that extra time. All the extra days a year that you spent sleeping, think what you could achieve with them? Whether it is planning to take over the world like Pinky and the Brain or exercising to give you more energy during the day. This morning period will put you back at the helm.

12

Energy Habits

The Habit Of Exercise

We all know the benefits of exercise. The feeling of well-being, the reduction in stress and the energy and vitality it brings our way. So why do so many people find it difficult to create a healthy habit of exercise?

Millions of adults are overweight and under-exercised! Millions more suffer from stress and anxiety. There is a simple solution for all of these conditions and it doesn't even require any financial investment. Exercise is as fundamental to happiness and success as oxygen. You rarely meet a runner who doesn't have control of their lives. Exercise is a keystone habit, a habit that enables other habits to form. If you start the habit of daily exercise you will find yourself with more energy, optimism and focus.

John's Story

The first time I met John he didn't stand out. He was one of a team of 10 and several of them were much more memorable characters. He contributed very little in the team workshop but I do remember one thing — the deep frown on his forehead. It was one of those frowns that I'm sure was incessant, unconscious to its owner, one that had been there so long that to the ones who knew him well, just saw it as part of his face.

A couple of weeks later I sat beside John for a one-to-one session. Often when I'm working with a team, I can sense the people who don't believe they need a coach. They are the individuals who are resistant to change. I expected John to be one of them.

To my pleasant surprise I got no resistance. It was a Monday morning at 8:30 and he was open and welcoming. He started by telling me a little about himself, his role in work and his life outside work. When he told me he was the father of three teenage boys and had a wife living with MS. Suddenly, the furrowed brow started to make sense. John described how he had been struggling since his wife was diagnosed. She seemed to be coping better than he was. He was feeling overwhelmed at work and his boys, like all teenage boys, were also a source of worry and stress.

We chatted for an hour and a half. We spoke about how he felt and how he could break free from his current overwhelm. He told me he used to go to the gym but since his wife had fallen ill, he had stopped working out. As a result, he had gained weight and was feeling tired and sluggish all the time. I asked him how he used to feel when he exercised. He described how his old gym habit used to make him feel great, it gave him a confidence and an energy he hadn't felt in a long time. He acknowledged that exercise was definitely missing in his life. That morning he committed to going back to the gym. He would start with three times a week and have breakfast with his boys the other two mornings.

Two weeks later I passed by his desk en route to meeting one of his colleagues. He looked up and smiled, a broad smile that carried up to his eyes. "I was at the gym this morning," he told me. He said no more but his eyes showed gratitude as he looked back at his screen.

Every day I meet executives who are stressed, who don't have time for exercise and my heart bleeds for them. I encourage, suggest and sell its benefits but it's a personal decision each person must make for themselves.

Other Benefits Of Exercise
You may think you know the benefits of exercise but that you don't have time for it right now. If exercises is not part of your everyday life you need to read on, exercise is not something you can put on hold, not only does it contribute to happiness but

is an important contribution to so many bodily functions. Read through the list of benefits and remind yourself how important exercise is for a happy and healthy life.

Happiness

Exercise is responsible for releasing endorphins into the brain. One of those endorphins is dopamine. Dopamine is a neurotransmitter that contributes to feelings of pleasure and happiness. It is the same neurotransmitter released in drug use. Serotonin also described as a happy hormone is not quite the mood-booster that dopamine is but more of a mood regulator, maintaining happiness rather than creating it. That is why an absence of serotonin is often related to depression. Most of the serotonin in your body is found in the digestive system. This is because serotonin is produced from the amino acid tryptophan, explaining why gut health and depression are also linked. Exercise and happiness are strongly linked.

Weight Loss

We burn calories when we exercise and to loose weight we need to burn more calories that we take in through food. But it's not just about reducing calories because if that was the case, if you simply ate less without exercising that would do the job too? The problem with that is you loose muscle as well as fat. When you reduce your calories, the body is forced to find other sources of fuel and ends up burning muscle protein as well as your fat stores. When you lose weight, you want to maximise fat loss and minimise muscle loss, this is what exercise helps you to do.

Increased Energy

Regular exercise increases your blood flow and your cardio-vascular health but how does it create more energy? The body stores and transports energy in your muscles using adenosine triphosphate (ATP). But ATP is not stored in cells so once a muscle starts to work, the body must quickly make more. One of the ways it does this is through aerobic exercise. When you start to exercise the body starts to supply your muscles with oxygen. When oxygen is present, aerobic respiration takes place and starts to break down the glucose for ATP. The glucose can come from food in your intestine, from the liver or from fat reserves. There are other more efficient systems that the body uses to create energy day to day and while ATP is the slowest of the systems, it can supply energy for several hours.

Reduces Risk Of Heart Disease
Regular exercise can lower blood pressure and reduce the strain on the heart. It also increases the good cholesterol that transports fat away from your arteries and back to the liver. It increases fat loss, improves circulation and builds muscle mass, all positive factors in avoiding heart related conditions.

Improve Your Focus And Memory
Exercise that elevates your heart rate can lead to improved focus and concentration. In a study carried out by the University of British Columbia, researchers found that that after a half hour of strenuous exercise, performance on tests of attention improves, problem solving and memory also improve. Apparently new brain cells are born in the hippocampus, the gateway to our memories, studies have shown that the hippocampus grows with exercise. As we know, memory fades with age so exercising regularly can help to counteract any memory loss.

Improves Your Sleep
Exercise appears to improve both the quality and duration of your sleep. When you are physically active you use energy, this energy expenditure means that you will feel more tired at the end of the day and ready to rest. It's important to note that it's not a good idea to exercise too close to bedtime. Your body temperature remains elevated for up to four hours after exercise, which could interfere with your sleep.

Reduces Stress

As you've already read, the endorphins released through exercise contribute to a sense of happiness and well-being, when you are in better mood you are less likely to focus on the negative aspects of your life. Along with this the actual exercise itself can act like a meditation, when you are exercising you are distracting your mind from your worries and focusing on the present moment.

Tips For Creating The Habit Of Exercise

* Start Small
* Choose something you like
* Create a schedule in advance — Monday, Wednesday and Friday at 6:30 a.m.
* Create a trigger — lay out running gear
* Track your success
* Mix your workouts if you start to get bored — run, cycle, tennis.

The Habit Of Healthy Eating

You are what you eat. Our bodies need fuel and the quality of that fuel will have an impact on your energy levels, your ability to focus, your decision making and your overall health and wellness.

With junk food so accessible and pushed at us through so many different mediums it can be very difficult to eat right all of the time. Creating good healthy eating habits will help you to ensure you make the right decisions about food as often as possible.

I have reduced my meat consumption by 90 percent. I decided to stop eating meat for both health and environmental reasons but was finding it difficult to have healthy alternatives all of the time. Eating out is especially challenging mainly because I also don't eat gluten so to find a healthy option that doesn't have meat or gluten can leave me eating convenience food that is not good for either my body or the environment. As a result, I decided to eat a little bit of meat when needs must.

In my opinion the 80/20 rule can be a good rule to follow when it comes to eating right. If you can fuel your body most of the time with the right foods, having convenience food and drink a small percentage of the time isn't going to be too damaging. I'm not a nutritionals and have no authority with my opinions on nutrition other than my own experience. Since I started to eat a healthy whole food diet, I have lost weight, have increased my energy and feel altogether better about myself.

Benefits Of Eating Healthy

Here is a recap on some of the many benefits of eating a healthy diet.

More Energy

Feeding your body with the right fuel will inevitably result in an energised body. If you are interested in high performance in sport or life you need plenty of energy to keep moving. To stay ahead of the crowd your energy must be top class and the only way to ensure this is through looking after your body. Ensure your energy habits are fuelling your body for success. Three meals a day won't be enough to stay energised. Eating smaller, more regular, meals will help you to maintain energy throughout your day and throughout your exercise sessions. This also helps to control your appetite and your metabolism. In my experience eating in this way helps me to maintain my weight and avoids that hunger binge at the end of a long day. High-protein snacks such as peanut butter balls, hummus, cottage cheese have all helped to curb the hunger and reduce the need for high carb snacks.

On a recent trip to a nutritionist with my son, we were told to include vegetables or fruit with every meal, as these are the life force foods. While at the time we were eating well it highlighted to me that we weren't getting enough natural foods in our diet. This will hopefully also increase your vitamin intake.

More Focus

Eating and drinking right will also help improve your ability to focus. Drinking sufficient water through the day will ensure your body stays hydrated. A dehydrated body means a dehydrated brain and a dehydrated brain will affect your memory and attention. As well as the fluids we intake the type of food you are eating will affect your ability to focus. Sugar, salt and artificial additives can all have a negative effect on your concentration levels and ability to do important work. A lot of the snacks we eat contain saturated fats and refined carbohydrates which do us no favours. As well as contributing to weight gain they also aid brain fog and lower cognitive function. So those cookies I ate on my tea-break were not a good idea. Diet drinks are also something you should think about eliminating from your diet. The artificial sweetener, aspartame has been linked to many damaging side effects, memory loss being amongst them. While its unclear if sufficient study has been done to verify the link, I for one plan to remove it from my diet. And of course the non-diet variety is not going to be a good substitute, the high levels of sugar give us sugar peaks and of course slumps. Sugar can be attributed to a brain fog that comes on after a mid afternoon binge of sweets treats.

Immune System Booster

We have long been aware of the connection between the immune system and food. Vitamin C probably still remains in the spotlight for immunity. But there are many foods that can keep the doctor at bay. Many of them — fruit and vegetables such as broccoli, red peppers and all of the citrus fruits. We also know ginger and garlic are powerhouses when it comes to keeping the colds away. Spinach our traditional super-food, turmeric the latest hero and green tea all have a claim on our healthy bodies and probably minds.

The best approach is to gradually introduce more and more healthy foods into your diet. Think twice about ordering a diet coke and substitute it with a sparkling water with lemon or lime. There are lots of healthy choices that can easily substitute your bad habits when it comes to food. The secret is to plan and prepare your food in advance. This will ensure you don't get caught out with only unhealthy options.

The Gut And Feeling Good

Increasingly the link between the gut and how we feel is being made. The Forced swimming test was carried out on some unfortunate mice. They were put in a container of water that was too deep for them to reach the bottom with their feet. This meant they were forced to swim around to keep afloat. Some mice didn't swim for long, they stayed still waiting for their fate, these are the ones with depressive tendencies. If these mice were given anti-depressants they would swim for longer. Irish scientist, John Cryan, took this experiment a step further and gave a group of mice good gut bacteria. These mice swam for longer with more motivation and their blood contained fewer stress hormones. In Guilia Enders book, 'Gut,' she speaks about further studies on the link between the gut and the brain which show that with a mix of healthy bacteria for the gut, areas of the brain were altered, in particular those responsible for processing emotion and pain. So eating right will not just have a positive physical effect on your body but can impact your emotions and wellbeing.

Tips For Eating Healthy

* Buy a healthy cook book with simple recipes and plan your meals
* Make a weekly shopping list according to your meal plan
* Buy healthy snacks such as nuts, Greek yoghurt and hummus and vegetables
* Pack a healthy lunch and snacks for work.
* Don't eat food out of a packet, put everything you eat on a plate.
* Don't skip meals, eat regular small amounts.
* Eat mindfully and savour each bite.
* Drink plenty of water.

Healthy Sleep Habits

Sleep is an important part of your maintaining your energy. If you don't get enough sleep your mood, concentration and motivation can suffer as well as it actually being damaging for your health. Sleep is a basic biological necessity for humans and essential for healthy body and brain function.

If you are suffering from lack of sleep you will not be able to perform at your best and it is not just the number of hours sleep that you get that is important but the quality of that sleep. If you sleep for ten hours but woke a couple of times during the night that won't give you the same benefits of having slept soundly for six or seven hours. The exact number of hours you sleep is up for debate but it appears to be veering towards eight hours as opposed to the once popular six hours for adults. Perhaps this is due to the quality of our sleep deteriorating due to excessive social media and electronic gadgets in the bedroom. Maybe it was always this way, but making sure you get enough shut-eye is vital for achieving your goals and performing at your best.

Benefits Of Adequate Sleep

Reduces Stress

A good night's sleep will help to reduce stress hormones in the body. If your body doesn't get enough sleep, it will be in a state of stress that may cause an increase in blood pressure and stress hormones. When your body has increased stress hormones it will be harder to fall asleep, therefore creating a loop of bad sleeping habits. To counteract and break the loop, you will need to introduce some relaxation techniques and create a relaxing environment for sleep.

Aids Memory

Sleep has been described as an energy-saving function as we restore energy resources, repair cell tissue and immune functions. But seemingly a loss of consciousness is not necessary to carry out these functions. This reinforces the supposition that sleep is also essential for the brain. Sleep is thought to aid memory consolidation and learning. While you are sleeping your brain is forming new pathways helping you to learn and remember information.

Health and Well-being

Sleep will impact your health and wellbeing in many ways. It is the absence of sleep where we will see the benefits of sleep, as lack of sleep can effect your health negatively in many ways. Sufficient sleep ensures the repair and maintenance takes place, hormones are regulated and proteins produced. Without sleep the negative impact will be quickly seen. Not only does sleep aid all the physical health but lack of sleep has also been linked to depression and a loss of well-being.

Weight control

Getting enough sleep is also linked to managing your weight. A study from Stanford University linked sleeping more with weighing less. The study showed that getting only five hours sleep is associated with a high body mass index. Being sleep deprived can affect your appetite hormones. If you are struggling to loose weight your sleep patterns may be having an effect.

We all know the benefits and have all experienced the undesirable effects. From lacking energy to feeling irritated and angry, none of the side effects are pleasant. If you have problems sleeping remember how powerful your thoughts are, if you believe you have a problem with sleep you do have a problem with sleep. If you want to impact your sleep you must start by implementing the good sleep habits below. These include not looking at screens for an hour before bed, not eating or drinking alcohol for a couple of hours before bed. See the other tips for sleeping better below. But you must also change the way you think about sleep. When you take positive steps towards changing something in your life — in this case sleep — you must believe that the changes you are making are going to have an impact. A bit like the placebo effect you have to believe it can change before it will change.

Tips For Healthy Sleep Habits
✱ Sleep in a completely dark room
✱ Keep the temperature low, a warm room will disturb your sleep
✱ Leave phones and gadgets outside the bedroom
✱ Don't eat for a couple of hours before bed
✱ Create a bedtime routine that is calming
✱ Keep animals outside the bedroom
✱ Try meditation or a relaxation technique before bed
✱ Begin Positive Affirmations such as below examples:
  "It's becoming increasingly easier for me to fall asleep and get a good night's sleep"
  "I no longer have sleep problems."
  "I love a good night's sleep and regularly get one."

13

Presence Habits

The Habit Of Meditation

I always knew that meditation was the answer to many of my shortcomings. I tried to do it at night but invariably fell asleep. I seemed to be under pressure for time in the morning, rushing to get the kids out of bed and everyone out the door. It took me a while to realise that I had to get out of bed earlier than my kids. Give myself plenty of time to fit in my meditation before they got up. It didn't always go to plan and often the little voices disturbed my quiet time but persistence was key and letting go0 of what didn't happen yesterday.

Have you ever been on a diet and eaten badly? What happens next determines your failure or success. Will you dismiss it and continue or will you tell yourself you've messed up so what's the point? Or maybe you've missed a couple of workouts and then you give it up all together telling yourself why bother? When it comes to habits you must stay in the present moment, each moment has equal value and isn't affected by what happened in the past. If you mess up, start again, if you forget, start again, if you are disturbed, start again. Each moment holds the point of power to choose how the future will look for you.

I have been meditating for about 10 years but only in the past two years have I established a consistent daily practice. Meditation is the one habit that I have mastered that I don't think I could ever live without. It's mind blowing to think that sitting in silence for 20 minutes a day can make you calmer, more focused, more compassionate and loving and overall happier and more successful. I know my energy has shifted and I know others can feel it too.

Benefits Of Meditation

The benefits of meditation span from physical benefits such as having a positive impact on blood pressure, the alleviation of pain in practices such as MBSR, (Mindful Based Stress Reduction) and decreased anxiety and stress. There are also the cognitive influences such as improved concentration and focus. Seasonal meditators will describe to you the subjective benefits such as inner peace and calm or clarity of mind, benefits that are not scientifically verifiable. But what is clear is that many meditators believe that meditation has contributed to more healing, happiness, flow and success, whether that can be attributed to the placebo effect or not who cares. The benefits are many and the time invested always appears to pay off in some aspect of life or other.

There are hundreds of studies that have been carried out on the benefits of meditation, here are just two of them.

Improved Focus And Attention

One study carried out in 2005 showed that meditation practice appears to be associated with changes in the brain's physical structure. Magnetic resonance imaging was used to assess cortical thickness in the study participants. What they found was that brain regions associated with attention and sensory processing were thicker in meditation participants than matched controls. The prefrontal cortical thickness was most pronounced in older participants, suggesting that meditation might offset age-related cortical thinning.

Reduced Stress And Anxiety

A study from the University of Wisconsin-Madison showed that the practice of Meditation (such as Vipassana), reduces the grey-matter density in areas of the brain related with anxiety and stress. Meditators were more able to "attend moment-to-moment to the stream of stimuli to which they are exposed and less likely to 'get stuck' on any one stimulus."

Here's what happened when a client started to meditate.

Ruth's Story

Ruth hired me to help her figure out her next career move. She was unhappy, stressed and overwhelmed with every part of her life. She held a very senior position in a well-known global entity. She was earning well over six figures and from the outside she seemed to have it all. Two beautiful kids, a husband who worked part-time and looked after the kids and the ability to work from home when needed. Truth was Ruth hated her job, everything about it made her skin crawl. She was working for a wage and she was dying inside.

She was afraid to move jobs as she believed every other job would bring its own level of politics and bullshit, and she needed the money. Ruth had financial problems brought about by her fathers death that left her cleaning up a mess that her mother was too old and fragile to be told about. The weight of the world was on her shoulders. Ruth was so stressed and wound up it took me a couple of session to start to unravel the false beliefs and negative emotions that she lived each day. Her thoughts were her own enemy and she could not see a way out of her current situation.

By the third session I was falling into the trap that a coach should always avoid. How can I fix this for her? When I realised where my mind was, I stopped myself, I took a deep breath and in that moment the word 'meditation' popped into my head. I asked her had she ever tried meditation and she said she had, but it didn't work for her. She said her mind was too busy and she couldn't stop her thoughts. I explained to her that meditation was not about stopping the thoughts but allowing them to drift away just as they had drifted in. I suggested a couple of sources for guided meditations which had helped me to get started with meditation and we parted ways. A couple of weeks later, I had my final session with her and while she said she had benefit from our time together I didn't feel she had.

Three months later I received the following email from Ruth:

Dear Ciara,

I've been meaning to write to say thank you so much for the excellent coaching sessions. It really was the best coaching I ever received. I appreciate your invaluable guidance and support in helping me to prioritise my goals and devise a plan to create a better life for me and my family.

Thanks for the tip on meditation, it's really helping. I feel so much more relaxed and my mind is clearer. I have decided to stay where I am for the moment but I no longer get caught up in the politics!

Thanks again for everything you have done,

Ruth

Different Types Of Meditation

It's important to remember that there are many different types of meditation and just because you have tried it once, doesn't mean that you cannot meditate. There are apps you can try such as Headspace and Andrew Johnson or you could try Deepak Chopra's meditation challenge. You can search YouTube for Body Scan meditations or Breath meditations. Keep trying until you find something that works for you. Meditation is a practice that will benefit your life in so many ways its worth giving it a go.

Tips For Starting The Habit Of Meditation

* Decide on a time of the day and stick with it
* Start small, even five minutes a day will benefit you
* Sit upright in bed, on a chair or a meditation cushion — don't lie down
* Don't try too hard — the aim is to let go of any expectations.
* As thoughts come, acknowledge them and let them go
* Breathe and enjoy.

The Habit Of Mindfulness

There is often confusion between what meditation is and what mindfulness is. Are they the same thing or do I need to practise both? Mindfulness is a type of meditation; living mindful is simply to live with awareness. It is bringing your attention to a particular object either real or in your mind. There are many types of mindful meditation, one you maybe familiar with is where you focus your awareness for a period of time on your breathe or you can do a body scan and bring your attention to each part of the body. You can practice mindfulness at any time of the day, stopping to bring your attention to what you are doing. When you do so, you are doing it in a non-judgmental way, simply observing the present moment.

Most of us spend our lives thinking about the past or planning for the future. Worrying, day-dreaming, plotting or planning. Rarely is our attention fully on what is happening right now. There's plenty of evidence to support that harnessing your mind to be in the present can improve your mental and physical health. Benefits include reduced stress and anxiety, positive thinking and improved mood.

Here are some mindful exercises you can do everyday:

Mindful Eating

A lot of us have an unhealthy relationship with food. We overfill ourselves with dinner, eat when we are not hungry and binge on chocolate and salty snacks while watching TV. But society is set up to tempt us to eat and drink at all times of the day. We associate relaxation with certain foods and drinks and stimulation with others. It's strange that eating has become such a source of misery in the developed world where we have an abundance of food.

Eating mindfully not only brings us back to the present moment, it also can improve our whole relationship with food, helping us tap into our body and listen to its needs. Mindful eating encourages us to simply witness the many sensations that occur when you are eating. Smell, sight, feeling all play a role in eating, but how often do we pay attention to it. Observe when the mind gets distracted, quietly coax it back without judgement. In this always on world, it's becoming less and less common to just sit and eat. We whip out our phones, stick on the TV or read while eating. When we do this we move our attention and awareness away from the food.

Here are a few ways to try out this mindful eating for the first time.

* The next time you drink a cup of tea or coffee, try and do so with your full attention.

* The next time you eat an apple, eat the full apple without doing anything else and paying full attention to its texture, taste and smell.

* If you are at work and tempted to eat at your desk, push the chair away from the desk or turn your monitor off for the time you are eating.

Try one or all of these simple techniques to get started. Remember to always start small and build on your habits rather than trying to do too much at once.

Mindful Walking

Mindful walking brings awareness to what is happening right now in your body and in your surroundings. Start with a deep breath, inhale, exhale and let go. Start to walk and bring your awareness to your feet, how does the ground feel underneath your feet? Open you senses and pay attention to your surroundings, see the light, the colours, the smell and the sounds, feel the temperature. Notice the air on your skin and connect with the air that surrounds you. Notice the trees, leaves and grass. Whenever you feel distracted bring your awareness back to the present moment and what you are experiencing.

This type of meditation can be done anywhere at any time of the day. Even if you are at work and moving between meetings you can bring your awareness to your walking. How does the ground feel beneath your feet? Mindfulness can be done at any time and any where and even if you only get to practice it for a moment it will benefit you. Try to practice every time the thought crosses your mind or when the realisation comes to you that your mind is somewhere else. Each time you recognise that you haven't been present, that in itself is a win, the witnessing of your lack of mindfulness is in fact being mindful.

Mindful Listening

How often do you truly listen to the person speaking to you? Listening is a skill not enough people are good at. We listen but our minds are always active, actively thinking about what we will say next or where we need to go next. Poor listening can account for a lot of conflict both at work and at home. When you only half-hear what has been said you won't see the full picture. Active listening means giving the other person all your senses. Often people say words that don't resonate with their body-language either consciously or unconsciously. Sometimes we convince ourselves that something is a good idea but it takes someone else to notice the incongruence of the words and the body. Next time you have a conversation with someone go into active listening mode. Attempt to listen with all your senses and get a true picture of what is being said. When you notice your mind drifting, acknowledge it, don't judge yourself but then bring your attention back to the person speaking.

Tips For Starting The Habit Of Mindfulness

✱ Commit to living your life more in the present moment
✱ Set reminders on your phone or on your computer (Where is your mind?)
✱ Start small and build up your practice
✱ Sit upright in bed, on a chair or a meditation mat (no lying down)
✱ Try a meditation app or follow a guided meditation on You Tube
✱ Breathe.

The Habit Of Gratitude

I first came across the concept of gratitude when I heard the word Mahalo. Mahalo like Aloha is a powerful and sacred Hawaiian greetings. Mahalo means "May you be in divine breath" and more common-place meaning is to give thanks for all that is, to show gratitude.

Gratitude is a powerful emotion and one that is the subject of many studies. Many scientists believe that the simple act of being grateful for what you have in life can enhance well-being, reduce stress and depression and overall make you a happier person.

In one study done by Dr Robert A. Emmons from the University of California and Dr Michael E. McCullough from the University of Miami, they asked participants to write a few sentences each week, focusing on particular topics. One group had to write down what they were grateful for during the week and the second group wrote about daily irritations. A third group wrote about events that had affected them, neither focusing on positive or negative events. After 10 weeks of this practice those who wrote about gratitude were more optimistic and felt better about their lives. This group also started to exercise more and visited the doctor less.

Dr Martin Seligman, a psychologist at the University of Pennsylvania, widely known as the father of positive psychology, included gratitude in one of his studies on positive psychology interventions. A group of people's weekly assignment was to write and personally deliver a letter of gratitude to someone who had never been properly thanked for his or her kindness, participants immediately exhibited a huge increase in happiness scores. This impact was greater than that from any other intervention, with benefits lasting for a month.

Karén's Story

A couple of years ago I met a wonderful lady by the name of Karen Dwyer as she competed in a speaking competition where I was helping out as a coach. Karen had a beautiful energy, authentic and raw, she told her story about her miraculous recovery from MS which she attributed predominantly to her daily practice of gratitude. Karen is a single mother of two gorgeous girls who after overcoming great adversity was diagnosed with MS.

After a couple of years on medication which she felt was having a more negative impact on her life that the MS itself, she decided to take full responsibility for her health so she quit the medication and made some changes to her life. She began a daily practice of gratitude by writing down three things that she was thankful for. Karen has created her own Gratitude Journal that you can find on http://mygratitudeattitudejournal.com.

In her case, a couple of minutes a day contributed to her turning her life around.

She suggests a morning practice upon waking. Practising gratitude at this time of the day can help to increase your mood right throughout the day.

I started to practise gratitude a couple of years ago and I noticed a big shift in the way I felt. Bad days weren't so bad when I remembered to be thankful. There are times in life that feeling grateful feels natural, your wedding day, the birth of a child or perhaps a good deed that creates a nice sense of well-being, but feeling gratitude when things are not so perfect, when you are experiencing the hum drum of life isn't such an easy thing. This is why having a daily practice can be so much more powerful, doing it every morning will keep it fresh in your mind and encourage you to do it right throughout the day.

Try creating a habit of gratitude, pick up one of Karen's journals or write it down in a simple notebook. Write down a list of the things you are grateful for. Your sight, your strength, your family and friends, not forgetting the things we often take for granted like our freedom to choose what we want. The feeling of the sun's rays on your skin or the privilege to breathe fresh air. A squirrel, a bird, a flower all the simple things that can bring us joy. Be thankful for the heating that turns on simply by pressing a button or the light that allows us to read into the night.

The more you practise the habit of writing down the things you are grateful for you will find yourself noticing more good things during the day. You will begin to notice how lucky and privileged your are and how a lot of your problems are insignificant in the bigger picture of life. There are many ways you can practise gratitude throughout the day, mindfulness, small acts of recognition and kindness.

Being grateful will change your life and touch the lives of those around you and the fantastic thing about this new habit, it will only take you a couple of minutes each day.

Tips For Starting The Habit Of Gratitude

✱ Make a gratitude list and look at it daily
✱ Get a dedicated journal and write down three things each day
✱ Set reminders during the day — "What are you grateful for?
✱ Include three things with your morning meditation.

The Habit Of Positive Thinking

Everyone has strengths and weaknesses. When it comes to our friends, we focus on their good points, the parts of them we like. If someone asked you to describe your closest friend, what would you say? She's kind, thoughtful, a great listener and fun to be around. You would rarely mention her weaknesses as that's not the way you think about your friends.

When it comes to enemies, we do the opposite, we mention all the reasons why we dislike someone and don't spend an instant pointing out that they too have positive personality traits. We often aren't so positive when it comes to describing ourselves or the lives that we lead. Some people are more positive than others, choosing always to turn negative occurrences into something positive. Others can't help themselves and choose to always focus on the negative, justifying their thinking by the fact that they're being realistic.

Positive thinking often gets bad press as being a soft and fuzzy attempt at happiness but it's the precursor to mental toughness, to confidence and to all success in life.

It all starts with a thought and that thought must be optimistic in some way if we are to believe that we can achieve it. Without optimism, you'd never start a business, get married or even have a child. Focusing on the positive is essential to achieve anything in life.

If you start to make a change in life without thinking that you can, you are wasting your time. If you mind is full of past failures, your supposed shortcomings or all of the potential barriers for success, you are putting yourself at a disadvantage. What about starting something with a positive attitude that we will overcome all adversity?

Barbara Fredrickson is a positive psychologist at the University of Carolina who has written extensively on how positive thinking can have a powerful impact on your life. Positive emotions such as joy and love appear to have a complementary outcome, they broaden thought action possibilities... in other words they broaden our thinking. Negative emotions such as fear and anger have the opposite effect, reducing our capacity to think of more options. So with positive emotions you will look at more options and see more possibilities in life. Fredrickson refers to this as 'the broaden and build theory' where you will build more skills based on the positive emotions felt while learning new skills. Analysis of a range of positive emotions support Fredrickson's claim:

Joy broadens skills by creating the urge to play, pushing the limits, and being creative.

Interest broadens by creating the urge to explore, take in new information and experiences, and expand the self in the process

Contentment broadens by creating the urge to savor current life circumstances and integrate these circumstances into new views of self and of the world

Pride from personal achievements broadens by creating the urge to share news of the achievement with others and to envision even greater achievements in the future.

Love broadens by creating recurring cycles of urges to play with, explore, and savor experiences with loved ones.

These various thought-action tendencies to play, to explore, to savour and integrate, or to envision future achievement represent ways that positive emotions broaden habitual modes of thinking or acting. So positive thinking is not a fluffy subject but one grounded in science.

Jason's Story

At 16, Jason was captain of his basketball team and very active in the community. At 17, he was Head Boy and destined for greatness.

The world was his oyster.

College years passed by uneventfully as he went thought the motions of a degree he had no interest in. The years passed and although he had no idea of what his future would contain, he knew in his heart that success was an inevitable part of that future. As the confident, relaxed person he was, he presumed life would fall into place, eventually.

At 30, with some achievements under his belt he started to feel dissatisfied, unfulfilled and a little disillusioned as his friends from school with much less potential and far fewer brains drove around in flash cars. He was driving a small hatchback.

"One of these days I will get noticed," he would say to himself but the years ticked on and nothing much changed. By this time he was self-employed, at least realising that he needed to take responsibility for his own success. Doing a bit of this and a bit of that, using all his technical skills to bring in the money, he continued to be a disappointment to himself.

When closer to 40 than 30, he heard a line in a song that was about to change his life. "Change will only happen when you change yourself." The words resonated deeply and stuck with him.

You see with the years of frustration and disillusionment came a little too much comfort-eating and a few too many beers any night of the week. Overweight and mildly depressed, he wondered why life had been so unfair, why had he not made it when so many others had? What was he missing? There must be a secret but he just hadn't figured it out yet.

He thought about this for a couple of weeks until he really understood what he had to do. He was tired of wallowing in self-pity and fed up of being mediocre so he decided to take action. He made a decision to change; to become a better person and surely then success would come his way.

Exercise, healthily eating, rising early, meditation and all sorts of personal development were on the agenda. He needed to clean up his act and get his life organised. Take control of his finances and finally make something of himself. Be the person that he knew he could be, someone his wife and children could be proud of.

The next morning he began to make those changes. He set the

alarm for 5am. Got up, exercised, tried to meditate and wrote in his journal. He worked for several hours, ate a healthy lunch and continued working in the afternoon. That evening he avoided his usual beer before dinner and decided to read a book on goal setting instead of watching TV. He read his kids a bedtime story, then went back to his book on goal setting, falling asleep at 9pm on the sofa exhausted from his new regime. The following morning the alarm went off at 5am. He hit snooze, next thing he knew it was 8am. Everyone was late for work and school and the house was in mayhem.

He felt disappointed with himself. "I knew I couldn't stick with it but I was worse than I thought. I only managed one day. I'm pathetic, a useless piece of shit." At lunchtime, he thought about having a healthy option but then he decided what's the point. That evening he went back to his old habits — his comfort zone of zoning out with a beer in front of the TV.

A month later something reminded him to give it another go, this time he decided 5am wasn't natural so he would try 6am and just exercise. For the next year, he started to focus on what he was achieving. This time, he wanted to recognise any wins rather than criticising himself for his failure.

After 18 months, he'd lost 10 kilos and had run a 10k race. He stopped calling himself pathetic and started to encourage himself with positive words. He continued to read personal development books and learnt to focus on the things he wanted in his life and not on the things he didn't want.

He began to write down his goals. He realised that he needed to be clearer about what he wanted to achieve to be successful. He understood that it was his own lack of clarity and vision that had held him back until now. He now knew that if he wanted to become the man he knew he could be, he had to take control of his life, his habits and his goals. What Jason realised was that when you are in a place you don't want to be, the clearer you get about where you want to be, the quicker you will be able to take steps to get there. And the more support you give yourself with positive thoughts and positive words the more likely you are to both achieve your goals and be a happier person.

Tips For Creating The Habit Of Positive Thinking

* Make a gratitude list
* Journal about the positive things that happen to you each day
* Create the habit of meditation
* Monitor your thoughts and replace every negative thought with a positive one.
* Challenge your negative beliefs every time you uncover one.

PART 4

Maintaining Momentum

The great thing about animals is that they generally allow evolution to happen... they don't resist it

14

We All Need Sticky Feet

THE native green lizards happily occupied the lower branches of Florida's trees. Scientist decided to invite their Cuban cousins to the party. Their cousins seemed to enjoy the lower branches too which led to limited space and food so the local green lizards decided to make a move.

They abandoned the lower branches and moved up into the treetops. But what they didn't realise was that up high in the treetops the branches were thinner and smoother. To be able to hang onto these smooth branches, the lizard's toe pads grew bigger and their scales got stickier. In just 15 years they got sticky feet.

Yoel Stuart, the main researcher who carried out the study in the College of Natural Sciences at The University of Texas at Austin said: "The degree and quickness with which they evolved was surprising," We have always thought of evolution to be something that happens over thousands of years and countless generations but these lizards adapted to their environment in just over 15 years and 20 generations. The great thing about animals is that they generally allow evolution to happen. They don't resist it. Imagine what would have happened if the little green lizard were stubborn like a human and decided that they liked the lower branches and they weren't moving for no one. Maybe they would have encouraged their brown cousins upwards or maybe they would have all suffered from limited resources and perished.

So take a look at your own life and ask yourself if you are resisting change from happening or if you are happy to get those sticky feet.

Overcoming Resistance

Imagine if everything you did each day, all your daily tasks required some thinking and decision-making. Imagine the cognitive load that you would place on your already hard working brain. What if you could eliminate the need to spend time on all low priority decisions, having pre-programmed your brain to look after them? By doing this you will have done your brain a big favour and increased your brains potential to focus on the big important decisions.

So why do we continue make our lives difficult by having to think about and make decisions on basic tasks and activities everyday? Why do we resist forming simple habits that can help us do things more quickly, more efficiently and make life much easier?

I have spent most of my life resisting habits. Being the youngest of six, I was rarely asked to help out at home. I grew up never having to do much of the daily routines and chores and when the moment came when they had flown the coop and it was my turn to help out, I didn't like it one bit. To this day I hate being told what to do. It's a character flaw I have been working on. I'm not completely closed to external input, I will happily take advice but tell me what to do and you will meet strong resistance.

I also bore easily; I seek the distraction of variety. This I have never found to go well with forming repetitive tasks. If I have to do the same thing every day for a month I guarantee you I will be looking for an alternative solution or a long haul flight to anywhere but here by the time day seven comes along.

To top it all I am a non-conformist. I don't like tradition or the status quo, never have and I don't think I ever will. Sending Christmas cards, going trick or treating, giving gifts on Valentine's Day, and all the other commercially created behaviours I don't buy into. But it's not just the commercialised ones I dislike, it's the religious and social norms society adheres to, because that's just the way it is.

The thing is, even in my personal extremes, I know I'm not the only one who feels like this. Resistance is not just something I suffer from, humans in general appear not to like being told what to do. We naturally resist change. We like to keep things just the way they are. We tend towards the path of least resistance; we like to stay in our comfort zones.

There are many ways in which we resist habit formation even without realising it.

Understanding Yourself

When I started to understand who I am and what I'm like, it became easier to overcome my resistance and understand that certain habits would enable me to change for the better. Recognising that changing my habits would be for my own personal good helped me to conquer my aversion to becoming part of a tribe that does things properly. Looking back at Chapter 2 and doing the exercise on beliefs will also help you to understand what you are thinking about the new habit you want to create and help you get to the root of your resistance.

Is It Fear Based?

Sometimes we resist change because we fear what it may bring. There was a time when I had a number of clients who came to me wishing to change jobs. They would tell me about all the reasons why they need to change but they just needed my help to make sure they were making the right decision.

Isabelle's Story

Isabelle came to me miserable and stressed out. She told me that she was only in the job a month and she knew she had to get out. It was five years later and she was still there. Why? Her reasons were as follows, it was a very well-paid job and she needed the money. As she had now been there for five years she had certain perks that she wouldn't have in another job. She said she had worked hard and by now had proven herself, as a result she had more freedom than she would have in another role. The fact was that Isabelle was highly qualified and highly employable she could probably pick up five jobs tomorrow at the same pay if not more. In the industry she was in and at the level she was at, freedom and flexibility would not be an outlandish request. As Isabelle spoke and rationalised her decisions and actions her body language and her facial expressions told the story. The job was slowly killing her inside. The culture of the company was not in alignment with her values and she went to work miserable each day.

Why did Isabelle like many others resist a change that would ultimately make her happier? Because she was scared, she couldn't get past her fear-based response. What if the new job was worse?

Anyone from the outside can see that the best outcome for her is to leave the environment that is making her unhappy. She herself knows this to be true but a fear she couldn't seem to overcome held her back.

We often stay stuck in our current world because we fear discomfort, we fear the unknown, we dislike the idea of having to continue with something that doesn't make us happy, the unknown brings with it so much more fear than the unpleasant current situation.

Unconscious Conditioning

Many of us have been conditioned not to ask for too much, whether it is your nations' culture or your religious upbringing there can sometimes be an implied greed associated with wanting more.

In the case of my client deep inside she believed that she should be grateful for the job she had. She was well paid and was able to support her family. She believed that she was being greedy and ungrateful asking for more. And what was she asking for? Simply her own happiness.

This was the essence of my religious upbringing; to be grateful for what we have. While in theory this philosophy appears sound, it also brings with it a nuance of don't ask for more than you already have, just be grateful for what you have and be thankful your situation is not worse than it is.

So when we set big goals, subconsciously we may be thinking should I not just be happy with what I have? Am I being too greedy? For years I has a subconscious belief that I couldn't have it all. If I were to earn too much money, maybe my kids would get sick. It was such a fear that I wouldn't even consciously bring it to mind.

This belief I know came from my upbringing, whenever I pined for more money my health was paraded in front of me, statements like the following: "Isn't health more important?" or "Your health is your wealth" or "There are so many rich people without their health." These statements were so common that the belief became a see saw. You could only have one or the other.

Ironically, my family had both money and health, but I made the association for my own wealth and health and somehow my brain skipped over me and focused on my children, I cannot be wealthy and have healthy and happy children. What a disastrous thought, but it was one that I carried around. Even as I write this, I am reminded of the anxiety it caused in my stomach and I have to remind myself that as I write, both my parents are financially comfortable and very healthy at age 83. I know that this false belief held me back for many years. Unconscious beliefs can be very limiting to happiness and success, so if you haven't done the exercises in Chapter 3 go back and do them to uncover your resistance and limiting beliefs.

Ticking boxes or putting a line through completed tasks puts you in a success frame of mind, assisting with motivation and overall success

15

Overcoming Procrastination

THERE are times when procrastination does no harm and can sometimes even be beneficial. On other occasions it can have damaging effects on your job, your relationships and even your health. Understanding why you procrastinate will empower you to recognise when it is damaging and make the necessary changes to stop doing it and start getting more of the right things done.

Procrastination Sources
Lacking Clarity

As mentioned earlier, clarity plays such an important role in our effectiveness and a major reason for procrastination can be the lack of understanding of what exactly is involved in completing a task. When a task appears too large; the thought of tackling it can be overwhelming. Spend a little amount of time breaking it down into manageable parts. Writing each step down and planning each step will give you focus and provide you with the opportunity to tick off each sub task as you complete it. Ticking boxes or putting a line through completed tasks puts you in a success frame of mind, assisting with motivation and overall success.

Lacking Vision

While lacking clarity may seem similar to lacking vision, when you lack vision you don't have any plan for the future that inspires you to move forward. If you lack vision, you can ask yourself the following questions. Where do I want to be in ten years' time? What do I want my life to look like?

In a work scenario, too many managers get caught up in the day-to-day activities that they forget to plan for the future. They allow themselves to become reactive, spending their day answering emails and attending to other people's priorities because they haven't established what their own priorities are.

Lacking Focus

Not having clarity about what you want to achieve leads to a lack of focus and a tendency to procrastinate on certain tasks. Many individuals don't understand their priorities, leading them to spend time on the wrong tasks. Get clear about your priorities. Don't spend your time working only on stuff that you enjoy, focus on your priorities will get you much better results.

Take control of your distractions, turn off notifications and remove yourself from temptation. Plan your environment to support you rather than hinder your success.

Lacking Energy

Life can be tiring, we all have so many responsibilities and feeling tired all the time can be an outcome of our busy lives. Tiredness can be a genuine reason for procrastinating. You finish a hard day at work, then you get home, have to cook dinner attend to children and a multitude of other responsibilities. By the time all the daily chores are done, you are too exhausted to do anything else. Lacking energy is real and can be a challenge. So what can you do about it?

If you lack energy, you need to look at your life and see what you can do to give you more energy. Very often, people don't exercise because they don't have enough energy. Remember that exercise creates energy and will give you that extra boost to get more done. All high achievers use exercise to enable their

OVERCOMING PROCRASTINATION

active schedules. A lack of energy can also be caused by a poor diet or lack of sleep. Decide what's contributing and make a decision about what you need to change to give you more energy and zest of life.

Start Small

One of the best ways to overcome procrastination is to start small. Plan a small action to get your going. Commit to doing one small action. Schedule five minutes in your calendar. Think of Isaac Newton and understand that once you start its easier to keep going than to stop. An object in motion will tend to stay in motion, so if you can take action with the 10-minute rule, you can create the momentum to keep things going. Making a start is always the most difficult part.

Anti-Procrastination Strategies
Unplug

I know it's easier said that done, the internet with all of its shiny information luring us there like a flock of magpies. If you really want something you have to become more conscious of what it takes to get it. Its back to the question what are you willing to give up to get what you want? You know if technology is holding you back or not. If it is, take action. At the weekends I often leave my phone in my bedroom, out of sight and out of mind. It sometimes amazes me that the day has passed and I haven't thought about it once. I have been more present and more relaxed. What also amazes me is that sometimes there is not one missed call or one message... life goes on without me. Switch off, turn off, unplug take some time to turn off notifications on all your social media platforms. Turn off your phone when you are trying to do focused work. Close your email and unplug the router. These are some of many simple steps you can take to reduce the distraction that may be causing you to procrastinate. It's easy to do when you make the decision to do it. Take action and take back the control of your life.

Practice Mindfulness

The more mindful you become, the easier it gets to focus. Becoming more mindful means that you stop letting life happen to you. You become more conscious of what's happening. What's working for you and what's not. When we procrastinate, we are often using distraction tactics to not think about the things that we know we should be doing. Mindfulness helps us face them. It helps us to be in the moment and if we decide that the moment involves procrastination, that's fine too. Being in the present moment is to enjoy it for what it is, to not think about the future or the past but you can only do that when you have faced up to do. Don't avoid, assess, plan and relax.

Subtraction Strategy

Often procrastination stems from overwhelm. In our over-stimulated world there is always more that we could be doing and more that we want to do. When I procrastinate, it is usually down to overwhelm. There are so many things I want to do I can't decide where to focus my attention. For this reason, the subtraction strategy has been a very useful strategy for me. What can I subtract, eliminate, postpone or simply dump from my life? I do this on a regular basis. From physical items such as clothes, books and accessories to work projects and commitments.

What's weighing you down?

I spoke about this a lot in my first book 'Chaos to Control' and in my online course. Creating a clutter-free world was so important to my advancement in life. Holding onto possessions that don't add any value to your life, is a waste of space and time. I regularly clear out my wardrobe and all of my cupboards upstairs and downstairs. It can be extremely cathartic. While I did this successfully for years, my books were not on the menu. I'd buy another bookshelf and my husband would reluctantly assemble it for me. He would softly suggest I dispose of the ones I hadn't read in a while and would I not give them away to charity? It was only when I read Marie Kondo's book 'The Magic Art Of Tidying Up' that I was able to say goodbye. She suggests that with every item we own we should ask the question — Does this spark joy? When I did this with many books the answer was an obvious no. I have kept the books that are relevant to my job, my reference books and the books that had a transformational effect on my life. They spark joy. But the countless novels and books that I bought because I thought I would read them, they all went. Eliminating the physical unnecessary items from your life is a great start to de cluttering your life and your mind. The next step is your work load.

When you are feeling confused, overwhelmed or frustrated with work, you need to sit down and take a bird's eye view of what's going on. I find a mind map to be very useful for this. Put down on paper all the different areas of work or responsibilities you are involved in and brainstorm what needs to happen in each area. This can be useful for work projects if you are employed or self-employed or even responsibilities and goals in your personal life. After mapping out all the different things you want to do, decide which one is most important to you.

Which one is going to advance your career?

Which ones are just nice to have?

Which ones are essential?

Sometimes, it's good to do this exercise with a friend or a coach. When you talk someone through your work, you'll sometimes find yourself justifying some parts of it. When you start to justify something, it's obvious you think it's not as important as other things. However, you may have a sentimental attachment to it or maybe you know it doesn't make sense in the material world but in the emotional world it's the only thing that matters to you.

The goal here is not to find the most practical, highest return on investment, (it may be for a work-related project) the goal is to understand your own priorities and make some decision about what's in and what's out for the next 3, 6, 9 or 12 months. Start to eliminate the least attractive, the lowest return on investment and anything that makes your toes curl up when you look at it! Don't do things because you think you should do them, do them because they make sense and you want to do them.

Best Year Yet?

The year 2008 was the first time I was able to look back and feel a sense of achievement. I had done what I had said I would do, achieved my goals and made progress in my life. It was my best year yet.

What's the one thing if you were to achieve would make this coming year one of your best yet?"

This question was what helped me write my first book, it helped me to create meditation as a daily habit and many other goals that have contributed to a life well lived.

Once you know what your main goal is, you will know what habit you need to create to achieve it. Motivation and focus then become a lot easier and procrastination a thing of the past.

Remember, your biggest enemy in this life is not your oldest rival but your inner voice...the one that makes you play victim to your circumstances. The voice that encourages you to stay in your comfort zone and remain mediocre. That voice is your arch enemy and you need to unveil and expose it.

So if you get out to run, rather than focus on the pain in your legs when you run, tell yourself you are amazing for getting out again today. You will feel great when you get home and into the shower. It's going to be a good day with lots of energy and focus.

Rather than think about how tired you are when you get up early, tell yourself 'well done' for rising before your bull. You are doing great.

Speak to yourself in the same way you would encourage a friend. Be proud of each day you manage to maintain your new habits.

There is a sense of control acquired from beating the inner voice. If your mind can win the daily battle between victim and success, things start on a high note and usually only get better. Recognising the voice is your best defence against it. When the alarm goes off and the voice tells you that you went to bed far too late to get up this early, or that five more minutes won't hurt, don't listen! Don't allow the voice to sabotage your greatness. When you are in charge of the inner voice, there will be no stopping you.

Rising early has thought me that if I can overcome my biggest challenge, change a habit that I thought was inherent, tied to my DNA, then I can do anything. It has injected a confidence into my veins that nobody can take a way.

So commit to 'Rising Before Your Bull' and creating the habits that will contribute to a lifetime of happiness and success.

Next Steps

There are several resources available to support you in creating your new habits:

Performance Scorecard
Take our Performance Scorecard and benchmark your habits for High Performance at *https://www.ciaraconlon.com*

Your Next Speaker
Hire Ciara to speak in your organisation
https://www.ciaraconlon.com/speaking

Your Coach
Need help unlocking your full potential
contactus@ciaraconlon.com

Online Programme
Register your interest for our online Habit Coaching Programme
contactus@ciaraconlon.com

Stay in Touch
t@ciaraconlon in@ciciconlon f@coachciaraconlon

About The Author

CIARA CONLON engaged in her first business venture at age 17, organising a clandestine end of school dance with her friend Derek. Because she used school property and the school intercom system to rally the troops, she almost got expelled on the penultimate day. The Head Nun told her as much when she said she didn't want to be responsible for having to expel the Head Girl.

Since then she has worked above board. She is currently a leadership coach, helping performers become high performers. She is an international keynote speaker. Her company 'Spirit Leadership' works with leaders and teams to improve well-being, productivity and performance. She has worked with organisations such as Deloitte, KBC, Savills, The Central Bank and Smurfit Business School. She is a member of the Professional Speakers association in Ireland and is regularly hired to motivate senior leadership teams.

Rise Before Your Bull is Ciara's third book. Her first book was 'Chaos To Control', a practical guide to getting things done. Her second 'Productivity For Dummies' published by Wiley 2016.

Ciara holds a BA Economics and Politics, A Master's degree in Business (Leadership, Management and Strategy and Innovation) Diplomas in Coaching and Organisational Psychology. She is a certified Mindfulness Meditation teacher and an Evernote Certified Consultant.

Ciara's goal is to bring more humanity into the business world and unlock the potential in everyone she works with.

Appendix A
The Habit Canvas

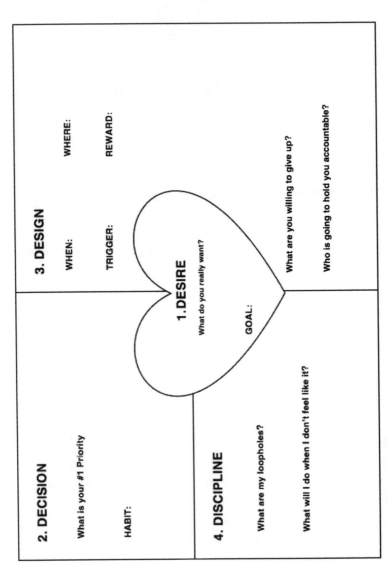

2. DECISION

What is your #1 Priority

HABIT:

3. DESIGN

WHEN: WHERE:

TRIGGER: REWARD:

1. DESIRE

What do you really want?

GOAL:

What are you willing to give up?

Who is going to hold you accountable?

4. DISCIPLINE

What are my loopholes?

What will I do when I don't feel like it?

5. ENVIRONMENT

Appendix B
Values

Take the time to work out what your values are, this will create clarity around your purpose in life and what you want your future life to look like.

Accountability	Consistency	Economy
Accuracy	Contentment	Effectiveness
Achievement	Continuous	Efficiency
Adventurousness	Improvement	Elegance
Altruism	Contribution	Empathy
Ambition	Control	Enjoyment
Assertiveness	Cooperation	Enthusiasm
Balance	Correctness	Equality
Being the Best	Courtesy	Excellence
Belonging	Creativity	Excitement
Boldness	Curiosity	Expertise
Calmness	Decisiveness	Exploration
Carefulness	Dependability	Expressiveness
Challenge	Determination	Fairness
Cheerfulness	Devoutness	Faith
Clear-mindedness	Diligence	Family-orientedness
Commitment	Discipline	Fidelity
Community	Discretion	Fitness
Compassion	Diversity	Fluency
Competitiveness	Dynamism	Focus

Freedom	Making a difference	Service
Fun	Mastery	Shrewdness
Generosity	Merit	Simplicity
Goodness	Obedience	Soundness
Grace	Openness	Speed
Growth	Order	Spontaneity
Happiness	Originality	Stability
Hard Work	Patriotism	Strategic
Health	Perfection	Strength
Helping Society	Piety	Structure
Holiness	Positivity	Success
Honesty	Practicality	Support
Honor	Preparedness	Teamwork
Humility	Professionalism	Temperance
Independence	Prudence	Thankfulness
Ingenuity	Quality-orientation	Thoroughness
Inner Harmony	Reliability	Thoughtfulness
Inquisitiveness	Resourcefulness	Timeliness
Insightfulness	Restraint	Tolerance
Intelligence	Results-oriented	Traditionalism
Intellectual Status	Rigor	Trustworthiness
Intuition	Security	Truth-seeking
Joy	Self-actualization	Understanding
Justice	Self-control	Uniqueness
Leadership	Selflessness	Unity
Legacy	Self-reliance	Usefulness
Love	Sensitivity	Vision
Loyalty	Serenity	Vitality

References

BOOKS
Dispenza, Joe, *Breaking the Habit of Being Yourself*
Duhigg, Charles, *The Power of Habit*
Enders, Giulia, *Gut, the inside story of our body's most under-rated organ*
Maltz, Maxwell, *Psycho Cybernetics*

STUDIES
Page 32: Neuroplasticity—a paradigm shift in neurosciences
Chakraborty R, Chatterjee A, Choudhart S, Chakraborty PK.. J Indian
Med Assoc 2007

Page 46: Your unconscious is making your everyday decisions
Marianne Szegedy-Maszak
http://www.auburn.edu/~mitrege/ENGL2210/USNWR-mind.html

Page 80: How are habits formed: Modelling habit formation in the real
world. Phillippa Lally, Cornelia H.M. Van Jaarseld, Henry W.W. Potts, and
Jane Wardle in 2010 in University College London

Page 86: Extraneous factors in judicial decisions
Shai Danziger, Jonathan Levav, and Liora Avnaim-Pesso
https://www.pnas.org/content/108/17/6889

Page 118: Effect of Exercise on Cognitive Function by Louis Bherer, Kirk
I. Erickson, and Teresa Liu-Ambrose
https://www.hindawi.com/journals/jar/2013/657508/

Page 124: About Sleep's role in Memory https://www.ncbi.nlm.nih.gov/
pmc/articles/PMC3768102/

RISE BEFORE YOUR BULL